Manish Singhal

Spirituality at Work

Manish Singhal

Spirituality at Work

A Study of Indian non-profit Organizations

LAP LAMBERT Academic Publishing

Impressum/Imprint (nur für Deutschland/ only for Germany)
Bibliografische Information der Deutschen Nationalbibliothek: Die Deutsche Nationalbibliothek
verzeichnet diese Publikation in der Deutschen Nationalbibliografie; detaillierte bibliografische
Daten sind im Internet über http://dnb.d-nb.de abrufbar.
 Alle in diesem Buch genannten Marken und Produktnamen unterliegen warenzeichen-, marken-
oder patentrechtlichem Schutz bzw. sind Warenzeichen oder eingetragene Warenzeichen der
jeweiligen Inhaber. Die Wiedergabe von Marken, Produktnamen, Gebrauchsnamen,
Handelsnamen, Warenbezeichnungen u.s.w. in diesem Werk berechtigt auch ohne besondere
Kennzeichnung nicht zu der Annahme, dass solche Namen im Sinne der Warenzeichen- und
Markenschutzgesetzgebung als frei zu betrachten wären und daher von jedermann benutzt
werden dürften.

Coverbild: www.ingimage.com

Verlag: LAP LAMBERT Academic Publishing AG & Co. KG
Dudweiler Landstr. 99, 66123 Saarbrücken, Deutschland
Telefon +49 681 3720-310, Telefax +49 681 3720-3109
Email: info@lap-publishing.com

Herstellung in Deutschland:
Schaltungsdienst Lange o.H.G., Berlin
Books on Demand GmbH, Norderstedt
Reha GmbH, Saarbrücken
Amazon Distribution GmbH, Leipzig
ISBN: 978-3-8383-7470-3

Imprint (only for USA, GB)
Bibliographic information published by the Deutsche Nationalbibliothek: The Deutsche
Nationalbibliothek lists this publication in the Deutsche Nationalbibliografie; detailed
bibliographic data are available in the Internet at http://dnb.d-nb.de.
 Any brand names and product names mentioned in this book are subject to trademark, brand
or patent protection and are trademarks or registered trademarks of their respective holders.
The use of brand names, product names, common names, trade names, product descriptions
etc. even without a particular marking in this works is in no way to be construed to mean that
such names may be regarded as unrestricted in respect of trademark and brand protection
legislation and could thus be used by anyone.

Cover image: www.ingimage.com

Publisher: LAP LAMBERT Academic Publishing AG & Co. KG
Dudweiler Landstr. 99, 66123 Saarbrücken, Germany
Phone +49 681 3720-310, Fax +49 681 3720-3109
Email: info@lap-publishing.com

Printed in the U.S.A.
Printed in the U.K. by (see last page)
ISBN: 978-3-8383-7470-3

Table of Contents

List of Figures

List of Tables

Dedication

To the loving memory of my mother

To my father, who lets me be

To my wife, but for whom this would not have been possible

To my sons Pankaj and Paaryah, for being themselves

Acknowledgments

It is only on occasions such as these that we realize the debt we owe to our past and to those who featured in it... those who enabled us to be who we are.

A thesis topic as personal as this brings back fond memories beyond the professional:

My uncle who with his wife left a thriving medical practice in the US to follow his Guru to India much before it became fashionable... He was my first brush with the power of spirituality over material aspects of life.

My mother whose indomitable spirit in the face of debilitating Cancer had her smiling till her demise...

My father who did not dissuade me from joining a spiritually-oriented service mission after my management education and instead encouraged me to follow my heart...

My friend Anand whose sense of community and unselfish spirit is an inspiration to me...

My colleagues at Vivekananda Kendra who helped me refine my thoughts and feelings in this area...

Professor Leena Chatterjee who defines an ideal teacher for me, someone I wish to evolve into...

Professor Amit Jyoti Sen whose engagement with philosophy led us to the deeper issues of research during our course-work stage...

Professor Surendra Munshi whose ability to place the most complex of ideas in the simplest of forms helped me at various stages of the doctoral process...

Professor B N Srivastava whose helpful nature I gained so much from during the data analysis phase...

Professor Sunita Singh-Sengupta whose faith in my potential was unwavering...

Professor Vidyanand Jha whose intellect I so admire and owe much to...

My dear friend Rajjog who lives the ideals I hold dear...

Debu-da with whom I grew up on this campus...

The FP students' community that helped me grow further... special mention due to Ganesh, Prem, Sangha-di, Madhushree-di, Shamama, Nilanjan, Rajiv-ji, Munish, Kirti, Vijay, Sumita, Nij, Sinna, Satish MK, Anshuman, Radhika and others who added various flavors to my stay at IIM-C...

Sandip of CMIE who helped me with SPSS and its intricacies...

Professor Sudip Choudhury who, other than his FPR Chair duties, took personal interest in helping us get a place to stay during the thesis winding up days…

Tapati-di, Mahato-da, Sushila-di and others at the FPM office who never let me feel that my problems were mine alone…

My brothers, in-laws, and other friends who put up with an erratic doctoral student…

Pawan prepared the software in which the survey data was fed… Pawan understood the change of specifications at the last moment and never complained…

Pandit-ji, though so far away, lent a helping hand when I needed it the most…

What do I say about Charu without whom I simply could not have come this far… she is a true life partner! Pankaj came our way mid-way through this process and filled our lives with so much of joy … He continues to teach me lessons in *tathātā* (present moment awareness)…

Finally, I would like to thank all the contact persons and respondents who patiently shared their lives with the researcher for this study… Swami Suhitananada-ji and Biswarup maharaj at Belur Math who opened many doors in the otherwise traditional Mission; Prof Ranjan Mitter whose sage advice revived my fortunes; Mrs Shubhra Chatterjee of Vikramshila and others who went beyond their call of duty to support an academic endeavor…

To all of them I owe this work.

Abstract

Spirituality at work (SAW) is an emerging research area in organization studies. It is being considered as a significant construct to deal with a number of issues resulting from increased dynamism in the business context and the resulting stresses and strains at organizational and individual level.

However, a review of literature in the area reveals that considerable challenges need to be overcome before these enthusiastic expectations can be realized.

Other than issues relating to the antecedents and consequences of SAW, major disagreements are the norm even in defining SAW. Scholars claim that innate ineffability of the construct makes it impossible to define SAW accurately. However, others equally emphatically assert that theoretical consolidation and advancement shall come about only after an agreed-upon definition emerges in the area. Further, panacea-like treatment of SAW disregards the contextual factors in the current SAW literature.

Based on literature review, this study argues that three features could be considered as central to defining SAW: Integrity/Wholeness, Meaningful Work, and Being Larger than Oneself. Further, this study proposed that the person-organization fit perspective from organizational behavior research could throw light on the under-theorized contextual focus in SAW research by providing a stronger link with SAW consequences.

Based on literature review, a conceptual framework for studying SAW was proposed. The framework linked individual SAW needs and organizational SAW supplies to emerge with a P-O fit on Spirituality at work. The individual SAW needs, organizational SAW supplies and SAW P-O fit were related to outcomes of Job Satisfaction and Organizational Commitment. In particular, the study examined the following questions:

1. What are the reasons for organizational employees to take up spirituality at work?
2. How is spirituality at work understood in Indian nonprofit organizations?
3. How is spirituality at work manifested and expressed in Indian nonprofit organizations?
4. Would a better alignment of individual SAW needs and individual perceptions of organizational SAW supplies be related to improved outcomes?
5. Does the organizational context mediate the phenomenon of spirituality at work and, if yes, how is the mediation effected?

The study used a mixed method strategy to enquire into the above research questions. The survey sample consisted of 179 respondents from six organizations (three each from the explicitly-spiritual sector and three nonprofits that did not have an explicit spiritual focus). Three survey instruments were used for data collection: self-designed P-O fit instrument on SAW, a modified version of Spector's Job Satisfaction Survey instrument, and a modified version of Meyer and Allen's Organizational Commitment instrument. Further, a semi-structured interview protocol was also utilized to address the research questions. In all, 114 respondents agreed to be interviewed for this study.

Statistical data were analyzed with SPSS 13.0 using descriptive, correlational, regression, ANOVA and MANOVA analysis procedures. One hundred and fourteen interview transcripts were analyzed using theory elaboration procedures.

Some of the significant findings of the study are given below:

Regarding the antecedents, the respondents did not agree with the position that the changed socio-economic conditions prompt the search for SAW. Instead, the influence of early childhood and family in inculcating appropriate values was seen as a greater force in motivating individuals to look for spirituality in later life. However, spiritually-disengaging influences in earlier organizations did prompt many to look for better opportunity structures for practicing spirituality at work.

The distinction between religion and spirituality that forms the basis for defining SAW for scholars did not find support in this study. This finding was linked to the cultural context where religion is more a way of life than a set of commandments to be followed. Further, the three-way conceptualization of SAW in terms of Integrity/Wholeness, Meaningful work, and Larger than oneself was supported in the study. Additionally, the respondents argued for including the practice component to the definition of SAW to focus on the need to engage in activities to sustain one's aspiration. That spirituality can not be demarcated in neat boundaries of personal and professional space was another strong finding from the study.

The study provides further proof that organizations need not necessarily constrain the expression of spirituality and may even provide facilitating conditions for its practice. At the individual level, the focus on self-transformation through work and progressive movement towards perfection could be taken as expression of SAW. At the organizational level, spirituality would be reflected in the underlying organizational philosophy which would be invoked to provide justification for each organizational activity.

The influence on outcome variables grew progressively stronger in this order: individual SAW needs, P-O fit on SAW, and organizational SAW supplies. Against the traditional focus on the individual to explain SAW processes and consequences, this study provides the first empirical proof of the interactive effects of individual and workplace spirituality on outcomes of interest to organizational scholars.

The study did not support the position that organizations could be neatly divided into "spiritual" and "not-spiritual" categories and instead suggested that organizations may be placed on a continuum of spiritual opportunity structures. Nonetheless, the explicitly spiritual organizations did overcome the spiritual practice versus performance focus by elevating ("Divinizing"?) the regular work done. Further, both in individual SAW needs and organizational SAW supplies scores the explicitly spiritual nonprofits significantly outscored their counterparts from the other category.

In terms of consequences, this study found that higher SAW scores were linked with higher scores of Job Satisfaction and Organizational Commitment. Qualitative data analysis suggested that individuals were able to overcome the material versus spiritual outcomes focus by linking the regular activities with an orientation that supported their higher aspirations.

The limitations of this study and implications for future research are discussed.

Chapter 1: Introduction

"There were two things I thought I'd never see in my life, the fall of the Russian empire and God being spoken about at a business school."

(Andre DelBecq, in Gunther, 2001)

"Organizations are constantly wanting and demanding more and more of us all of the time. But they can't have it both ways. They can't have more of us without getting and nourishing the whole person. Organizations must give back and contribute as much to the whole person as they want in return."

(A corporate manager, cited in Mitroff & Denton, 1999a)

Spirituality at work (SAW hereafter) appears to be an idea whose time has come. Since the late 1990's when the idea first started being mentioned in academic circles, the last few years have seen increasing academic interest in a concept that was hitherto relegated to the personal or religious domains. Not only has spirituality been vigorously discussed in popular literature, more and more academic journals and books are exploring a phenomenon that has apparently captured public imagination. In the next section the reasons for growing attention to spirituality at work is examined.

1.1 The Growing Relevance of Spirituality at Work

In this section the forces and conditions that have contributed to the emergence of SAW in academic literature shall be examined.

A number of changes in the environment over the last few decades have altered the way business management works today. Increasing globalization with the associated focus on off-shoring, de-regulation of markets and the allied advent of common markets, advances in technology, changing demographic profile, intensified competition, shift of focus towards the service sector—all these factors operate at many different levels and give rise to significant challenges for the management of organizations (Burke & Cooper, 2006).

Emphasis on knowledge-work in growing sectors of the economy, a salient feature of the new organizational context, places the employee at the heart of the organization. At another level, sharply accentuated mobility in labor markets and enhanced employment options have made the employee attraction and retention issues challenging for management. The situation has not been helped by the frequent re-engineering, de-layering and downsizing in organizations that has led to a trust deficit in the organizational climate. The erstwhile employment contract, which promised employee loyalty and commitment in lieu of job security, too does not appear to work any longer. Corresponding lack of employment security and heightened uncertainty has led to decreased morale, increased anxiety and an elevated stress response in the workforce today. Not surprisingly, the employees who constantly battle the fear of being laid off suffer from a diminished sense of self and seek a more stable source of meaning and purpose (Ali & Falcone, 1995).

In view of the many corporate scandals in the recent past, a growing emphasis on values and ethics is another prominent feature of the new workplace (Paine, 2003). Many authors also argue that corporate values have undergone a shift globally. Starting with corporate social responsibility movement, authors see evidence of more environmentally conscious and socially responsive organizations which are concerned with more than merely material assets (Wagner-Marsh & Conley, 1999). Perennial questions like "What is our purpose?" "What do we believe in?" "What principles should guide our behavior?" are being increasingly voiced inside organizations (Paine, op.cit.: 1). Alongside, there has been a proliferation of philosophies and holistic methodologies that advocate an integration of all aspects of one's life from leisure to work prompting individuals to explore Spirituality at Work (Cavanagh, 1999).

In view of all the above factors, SAW presents itself as an option that would not only promote employees' devotion to whatever activity they are involved in at work but would inspire them to identify themselves with their organization (Svejenova, 2005).

Complementing the beneficial organizational consequences from the practice of SAW assertions, a few scholars relate the practice of SAW to its traditional individual focus. These scholars put forward spirituality as the very core of life (Pargament, Magyar-Russell, & Murray-Swank, 2005) and accredit a more fulfilling, meaningful life to its practice. Thus a concept that was hitherto linked to the personal and individual aspect of one's life is at once brought out in the public and the organizational domain.

Consequently, there is a greater visibility today for articles on spiritual themes in business periodicals and academic journals, management development workshops that address spiritual themes explicitly (Bell & Taylor, 2004) and various conferences and workshops on spirituality at work.

However, the surging interest is spirituality at work has outpaced the capacity of scholars to keep pace with the construct either conceptually or methodologically (Giacalone & Jurkiewicz, 2003b). A number of such debates remain far from being settled as shall be seen in the subsequent sections.

1.2 Central debates in SAW

Amongst the major debates that have exercised SAW scholars has been the issue of SAW's antecedents. While many scholars refer to the works of Weber, Follett, Maslow and Greenleaf (Bell & Taylor, 2003; Casey, 2004; Quatro, 2003; Russell & Stone, 2002) to support their claims of such concerns having always been present in organizational literature, others cite the discontinuous change in the business environment as the major impetus for SAW's emergence into academic enquiry.

A central issue under the academic lens has been pinning down the very concept of spirituality at work! The disquiet about engaging with SAW in academia emerges partly due to the whole gamut of issues being subsumed under the concept: from a search for meaning, purpose, wholeness and interconnectedness at work, incorporation of yoga and meditation routines in organizations, SAW has also been argued to include such practices as feng-shui and reiki (Laabs, 1995). Quite understandably, scholars are at a loss as to what to make of a phenomenon that can be taken to mean anything and everything which contributes to employee and organizational well-being. The boundaries of the concept are rather indistinct in present-day literature and require clarification.

While a few scholars attribute the definitional multiplicity to the highly subjective nature of SAW and claim that trying to define SAW before initiating research would be counter-productive to the attempt of researching into the concept (Dean, 2004), Mitroff (in Dean, 2004) argues that an '"obsession" with finding a single correct, overarching definition of workplace spirituality does not respect the myriad traditions and belief systems embedded in our research arena.' A number of authors argue that the ineffability of the concept makes precise definitions inoperable (Chakraborty, 2004; Gull & Doh, 2004) and another section claims that "is not so much elusive and intangible as confused and imprecise" (Brown, 2003) to assert that not defining SAW makes it impossible to compare the findings from different studies (Giacalone & Jurkiewicz, 2003b), a step necessary for theoretical advancement.

A middle path has of late been suggested in literature: identification of a few central themes from literature could be taken as a starting point which could then be augmented with inputs from empirical enquiry (Dean, 2004; Dean, Fornaciari, & McGee, 2003). A promising lead in this direction appears to be the conceptualization of spirituality as a multi-dimensional construct (Hill et al., 2000b; Milliman, Czaplewski, & Ferguson, 2003) which would permit a profile analysis of each element individually - and all elements collectively - as a fruitful way of studying the phenomenon.

In this direction, a conceptual convergence has been detected in SAW literature that sees the varied understandings leading to a few common themes that largely accommodate the varied interpretations of the concept. However, while a conceptual convergence of the various SAW themes has been talked about in literature, an empirical validation of this assertion is lacking. This is one area of literature that this study seeks to contribute towards.

A long-standing distinction has been central to the very concept of SAW: the perceived similarity between the constructs of religion and spirituality! Religion has traditionally been construed as being divisive and unsuitable for secular organizational affairs and the SAW scholars too have largely treated spirituality as *non-religion* (Harvey, 2001). However, a growing body of literature asserts that the two constructs essentially speak about the sacred and are inherently intertwined making a neat separation counter-productive (Hill et al., 2000b; Pargament et al., 2005; Zinnbauer, Pargament, & Scott, 1999).

Drawing from the debated antecedents of the SAW movement detailed earlier, scholars have also argued on who drives the SAW movement: the organization or the individual. This question is considered important, as the response would indicate as to which outcomes could be deemed as being of primary importance. The employee-pull section of literature places the primary responsibility on the shoulders of individuals (Ashar & Lane-Maher, 2004;

Mitroff & Denton, 1999a; P. Vaill, 2000) even as the organization-push section bases itself on the benefits that can be derived by the organization if only the SAW initiatives were to succeed (Forray & Stork, 2002).

The instrumental, material purposes for which spirituality is being invoked inside organizations comes across as the next major debating point in SAW enquiry. The essentially non-material nature of spirituality is argued to militate against the associations with organizational profitability and growth (Benefiel, 2003; Tourish & Pinnington, 2002). However, others are equally convinced that till it is only by identifying SAW's practical implications that its utility can be demonstrated and its practice adopted by managers. If scholars fail in demonstrating the benefits that may accrue from SAW practice, the potential gains from SAW may perhaps never be realized (Giacalone & Jurkiewicz, 2003b). In continuation with the theme, it has also been argued that while corporations may begin with selfish ends in pursuing SAW, those objectives themselves may undergo a transformation if SAW is sincerely pursued (Benefiel, 2005).

SAW has been largely considered context-free and its benefits are argued to accrue to all regardless of the idiosyncratic contexts that organizations provide. This uncritical acceptance of panacea-like application of SAW to cure all organizational and individual ills disregards the intriguing interactive effects of personal-workplace spirituality (Jurkiewicz & Giacalone, 2004) and also undervalues the contributions of organizational contingency factors.

1.3 The Evolution of SAW Research Methodologies

Scholars have argued that SAW research constructs resist quantitative and positivist methods (Dean, 2004; Dean et al., 2003; Fornaciari & Dean, 2001), even as others (Gibbons, 2000b; Mitroff & Denton, 1999a) point to the lack of empirical literature on this topic. The tensions between conducting responsible empirical research and not trivializing deep spiritual traditions (Benefiel, 2003) are seen to pose difficult choices before any SAW researcher. A number of epistemological and methodological challenges in the field need to be overcome for the field to advance to theoretical maturity (Dean et al., 2003). The suggestions that have been offered include a preliminary identification of definitional elements; an openness to utilize both qualitative and quantitative methods to do justice to the inter-disciplinary concept; and finally, research to further develop the basic themes and a research agenda. A detailed analysis of these themes and their utilization in this study shall be taken up in later chapters.

1.4 Rationale for the Research

Given that the field of SAW research has not yet attained theoretical maturity (Jurkiewicz & Giacalone, 2004), and that it poses significant challenges for research (Dean, 2004), why is it still an interesting area for doctoral research?

This question could be looked at from two different perspectives. One way to answer this question would be from the practitioners' point of view where the utilization of SAW is expected to provide answers for many an issue that both individuals and organizations are struggling with. Secondly, in terms of theoretical contribution, a study that helps clarify the boundaries of the concept, examines the impact of the context in applying SAW and proposes and empirically tests the as yet under-theorized assertions about the potential utility of SAW in organizations would further confirm the potential of this construct.

At one level, growing turbulence in the business environment and an emphasis on knowledge work makes the need for a more vigorous employee engagement in organizational activities inevitable. Organizations today are looking for solutions that would help them engage employees without denting the organizational need for employment flexibility. Faced with a widening trust deficit in the wake of frequent corporate restructuring in the recent past, managers assume that a basic notion of SAW could act as "the common ground for the new work community" (Jerry Biberman & Whitty, 1999). In this context, SAW appears to be a prescription made to deal with these conflicting demands. From the individual's point of view, since spirituality is argued to be the very essence of one's being human (Mitroff & Denton, 1999a) scholars assert that allowing its expression would make the regular work seem more meaningful and purposeful.

At the theoretical level, as argued earlier, the existing literature on SAW leaves a number of issues that could have exciting implications for the concept's applicability inside organizations. The focus of this study on SAW conceptualization and definition, SAW manifestation, the interactive effects of individual and workplace spirituality, the effect of organizational context in SAW application, and the attendant benefits at individual and organizational levels would help in theoretical consolidation and thus advance the process of theoretical maturity.

1.5 Summary and Dissertation Structure

The present chapter explained why Spirituality at work is an important emerging area of research. It highlighted the major debates in this emerging area of organizational enquiry and pointed out the unsettled issues that shall be elaborated upon later. It then examined the evolution of SAW research and summarized the various suggestions for overcoming the present problems in an empirical enquiry. The chapter also presented a preliminary rationale for the study discussing its potential utility in terms of theoretical contributions and managerial implications.

A detailed literature review in the area of spirituality at work and the central debates that characterize the field is presented in Chapter 2. Firstly, this chapter examines and documents the growing interest in the field of SAW. Next, a summary of some important research in the area is presented with a critical review. Theoretical gaps and inconsistencies are highlighted to lead the way to a conceptual framework in the next chapter.

Chapter 3 builds up a theoretical argument addressing the gaps and inconsistencies identified, by drawing upon past research. This leads up to the formulation of research questions, and specific propositions to be tested by the research.

Chapter 4 presents the research design and the framework for the analysis of data. The research methodology, sample selection criteria, and data collection techniques will be discussed in detail in this chapter.

Chapter 5 presents the analysis of the data collected. The data collected using structured questionnaires was analyzed using statistical tools, and the major findings have been presented using tables and graphs. The qualitative data from 114 interviewees was content-analyzed and relevant themes are reported. The interpretations and implications of the analysis in the context of previous research in related areas is discussed in Chapter 6. The chapter ends with implications for future research and for practitioners, as well as the limitations of this research.

Chapter 2: Literature Review

Chapter 1 presented a preliminary argument for exploring the trend of 'spirituality at workplace' (SAW, hereafter) which has been posited as the device to find meaning and purpose in the workplace. Today, with the individuals looking for meaning and purpose in organizations, organizations themselves see SAW as a major resource to deal with an increasingly turbulent environment.

This chapter reviews academic literature from the nascent field of SAW and draws potential research directions relevant for the above-mentioned purpose. Firstly, the growing interest in the field is documented, which includes both the scholarly attention that it has received and what is apparent in popular writings. Secondly, the varied sources credited with resurgence of organizational interest in a concept that was hitherto relegated either to the religious domain or to the personal are identified. The third major part of literature review examines the central debates that have characterized the SAW discourse. These include the religion versus spirituality dichotomy that characterizes much of SAW literature, the difficulties with defining the ineffable spirituality, a conflicting view on who drives the SAW movement – the individual or the organization, followed by the disregard of context in SAW literature, and lastly, the contested SAW outcomes. The gaps identified in literature shall lead to the conceptual framework to be presented in Chapter 3.

2.1 Growing interest in Spirituality at Work

For the last few years, there has been an upsurge in interest in matters spiritual in the business domain reflected in practitioner and academic circles alike. Spirituality, until now relegated to the personal or religious domains of an individual's life, is increasingly coming into focus in the workplace. Many corporations are now explicitly using the word "spirituality" in their internal and external literature including Boeing, MacDonald's, American Express, SAS, ServiceMaster, Southwest Airlines, and Marriott. Further indicators of this rising interest include the growing number of sessions at the Academy of Management annual meetings that focus on this intersection of spirituality and managerial roles, an abundance of books – both popular and academic – addressing the issue, and relevant new courses and executive development programs being offered in business schools.

The most significant academic indicator of this newfound interest is the constitution of an independent special interest group on Management Spirituality and Religion (MSR) by Academy of Management (AoM), in 1999. The MSR preamble states:

> The primary purpose of the special interest group is to encourage professional scholarship in the relationship between management, spirituality and religion. The domain of this special interest group is the study of the relationship and relevance of spirituality and religion in management and organizations. Encouraging and conducting research; promoting the interchange of ideas, research, and other information; providing for fellowship among persons with professional interest in these areas; and engaging in other activities and services of interest to the membership are amongst our highest aspirations.

The formation of the MSR interest group is considered significant (Neal, 2000): "[AoM] is the most prestigious academic organization in the field of management, and they basically decide what is acceptable in the field and what is not. By approving this new interest group, the Board of the Academy is saying that spirituality in the workplace is a legitimate field of study and that research, teaching, and publishing are acceptable in this area."

Further, a broader avenue of peer-reviewed academic journals and conferences has become available to channelize the research output from academicians. Several journals have published special issues on the theme, including Journal of Managerial Psychology, Journal of Organizational Change Management, Organization and The Leadership Quarterly, amongst many others. Moreover, stray articles have also appeared in other journals such as Academy of Management Executive, Human Relations, Human Resource Development International, Organization Science, Organization Studies and Strategic Management Review. In addition, incorporation of SAW in standard organizational behavior textbooks too validates the perception that it is being considered mainstream today (Dent, Higgins, & Wharff, 2005).

Moreover, this growing interest is not limited to the researchers and academicians alone. They only seem to be documenting a practice that is becoming ubiquitous enough to be documented by popular business magazines like *Newsweek*, *Business Week* and *Fortune*. Growing demand for spiritual management development (SMD, hereafter) programs, attracting participation from corporate executives at all levels, illustrates yet another evidence of the growing executive need for and legitimization of spirituality in the workplace (Bell & Taylor, 2004). SMD, being premised on "personal and corporate salvation", employs a discourse based on self-fulfillment, self-discovery and self-development in relation to managerial work (Bell & Taylor, 2004: 441). While these programs amongst the corporates would have seemed strange earlier, their legitimacy today is reinforced by "academic and practitioner interest in the broader topic of workplace spirituality" (Bell & Taylor, 2004: 443). Having seen the growing popularity of SAW in academic and practitioner fields, attention shall now be directed to tracing the contentious issue of historical development of this discourse.

2.2 SAW's development: Spontaneous expression versus historical inheritance

While there are many who argue that the emerging SAW movement reflects a spontaneous concern with finding purpose and meaning in the workplace today owing to the changed socio-cultural and economic reasons, others feel that the academic movement derives much from long-standing academic traditions in organizational studies. Further, they argue that locating the discourse in the existing theoretical backdrop would help the movement gain its rightful place in academic circles. These two sets of rationalizations shall be explored below.

The spontaneous class of explanation offers socio-cultural, organizational and individual categories of reasons to explain the rising interest in SAW.

The various sociological and cultural factors that are argued to have prompted SAW are increase in leisure time, improvement in communication channels and wider access to technology (Neck & Milliman, 1994). These changes prompt the individual to look for fulfillment not only in the personal domain but also in their professional lives. Echoing the argument, Maslow's hierarchy of needs' theory is applied to the social level to claim that the improvement in economic condition has meant that an entire society has moved beyond its safety and security needs to look for satisfaction of higher-order needs (L. Tischler, 1999). From social movement along Maslow's lower order needs to the higher, some SAW scholars also take the leap to argue that the society itself has moved beyond the rational domain to seek trans-rational sources of fulfillment (Ashar & Lane-Maher, 2004; Bell & Taylor, 2004; Casey, 2004; Giacalone & Eylon, 2000; Tourish & Pinnington, 2002). The claim common to all such arguments is that the earlier assumptions of autonomous rational actors aiming at utility maximization do not work in a changed society where individuals value relationships, harmony, balance, and meaningful work. The paradigm shift argument "contrasts the old paradigm, which comprises mechanistic, dualistic, objectivist assumptions common to Newtonian science, against the new paradigm thinking, which is seen to be more inclusive, holistic, integrative, ecological, and empowering" (Lichtenstein, 2000: 1337).

In the context of business management, it is claimed that the old mechanistic paradigm led to a hierarchical organizational structure that operated through command and control. Individuals were expected to be mere cogs in the wheel and "check in their feelings, emotions, discretion, curiosity, and creativity at the office's door" (Ashar & Lane-Maher, 2004: 251). However, the new global economic order is based on knowledge, intelligence, and innovation where the command-and-control mechanisms operating earlier do not yield the desired results. In an economy where the human capital is more important than ever before, a company's continued success is determined by its ability to tap its employees' commitment, responsibility, creativity, and energy for which the organization needs to "nurture relationships and cultivate the human spirit" (Ashar & Lane-Maher, 2004:251). The changed economic order forces companies to integrate purpose and vision into business practice and acknowledge the spiritual dimensions of work. The same socio-cultural drivers prompt the employees to choose vocations that help serve the cause of personal development and integrate the personal and professional in one's daily life (Lichtenstein, 2000:1342-1343).

It is based on such observations that scholars claim that the earlier mechanistic world-view with its associated values, assumptions and practices is not operative in the 21st century organization and thus call for a more holistic approach to managing organizations (Ashar & Lane-Maher, 2004; Paine, 2003). Thus, the paradigm shift argument clearly sees the SAW movement as the need of the hour helping fulfill the operative social needs.

From the wider socio-cultural factors that have led to the prominence of SAW discourse today, there are narrower organizational issues that are claimed to contribute to the same phenomenon. A number of reasons are offered for this claim. An unstable work environment, characterized by frequent lay-offs, restructuring and various managerial measures that cut costs at the expense of employees have led to the situation where employees are distrustful of management (Cash & Gray, 2000). The distrust manifests itself in the breakdown of the psychological contract valid earlier where loyalty was traded for employment security. The demoralized workforce that results through this process has heightened fears of social alienation and fear, leading the employees to re-examine their values and search for deeper meanings in their lives (Giacalone & Jurkiewicz, 2003b). Further, the changed global economic order referred to in the earlier section highlights the critical nature of maintaining high organizational commitment for continued organizational competitiveness even when the dynamic business context does not allow the luxury of employment guarantees (Burack, 1999; Mitroff & Denton, 1999a). It is in this context that the organizations are claimed to have taken up SAW as the tool to heighten devotion to the corporate ideal (Tourish & Pinnington, 2002).

The increasing interest in the SAW discourse today has also been attributed to personal factors. One of the common explanations at this level is the exposure to new age philosophies and eastern religions that fuel the need to find meaning and purpose in the workplace through a deeper engagement with one's work (Ashmos & Duchon, 2000). Further, another contention that closely mirrors Maslow's hierarchy of needs concept argues that the improved material wealth and security prompts the search for alternative sources of meaning leading individuals to a more altruistic, expressive set of principles (Bell & Taylor, 2004). This claim pre-supposes a latent spiritual need in employees that can be fulfilled in the workplace, a claim found to be consistent with data by Ashar and Lane-Maher (2004). Ashar and Lane-Maher (2004: 252) sought to validate the frequent assertion in SAW literature that employees today desire a workplace that incorporates spiritual principles such as a focus on "relationships, harmony, balance, and meaningful work" through in-depth interviews on the concept of success with 49 mid- and senior-level executives in a US federal government agency. While religion, spirituality, and meaning were not explicitly mentioned in the study by either the researchers or the participants, the themes that were most frequently related to success mirrored the aspects related to SAW: integrity, wholeness, inter-connectedness, transcendence, and contribution to community and colleagues.

The three categories of explanation– socio-cultural, organizational and personal – summarized above assume that the changed environmental and individual factors are responsible for the upsurge in interest in SAW. This section of literature thus denies the possibility that similar concerns may have been present earlier in the organizational discourse and been accommodated by organizational theorists. However, a few studies (See Quatro, 2004, for an illustrative example) supplement the majority view of spontaneous expression to maintain that the SAW movement ought to acknowledge its intellectual debt to earlier scholars. They argue that SAW literature is only following in the footsteps of illustrious scholars who had earlier either foreseen the need for such a movement, or had made allowances for its emergence in their theories. References to a few salient theorists who had explored similar issues in their writings is detailed below to establish that such concerns and their accommodation is not new to organizational literature.

2.2.1 Max Weber

Max Weber, one of the founding fathers of the discipline of sociology, is well known for his *Protestant Ethic* thesis in which he argued that specific beliefs and attitudes characteristic of a protestant work ethic had led to the emergence of capitalism in the western world. Foundations of religious Calvinistic beliefs were claimed to have led to financial success of protestant enterprises in the western world.

Rejecting the claim that the current SAW discourse is either novel or breaks fresh ground, Bell and Taylor (2003: 344) link it explicitly with Weber's conception of religious underpinnings of commercial enterprises:

> One of Weber's central conclusions was that the spirit of capitalism would come to dominate as an ideal, and religious beliefs would be replaced by the pursuit of wealth and possessions. Weber's proposed solution to the iron cage of production and consumption therefore relied on the development of a sense of vocation and existential dignity within an ethic of individual responsibility; the individual could thereby mediate the alienation of rational labour. The workplace spirituality discourse shares Weber's acceptance of the structural conditions of capitalism and seeks to resolve the dilemmas these create for the individual by developing an inner sense of meaning and virtue. In this respect, workplace spirituality represents a return to or even a revival of the Protestant ethic, not as a way of life defined in terms of thrift and guilt, but as a means of living with capitalism through conscientious consumption and love of the self.

The only change that has come about in the argument, claim Bell and Taylor (2003: 345), is that Weber's protestant ethic has been remodeled to mirror the current sensibilities better: "…the discourse of workplace spirituality provides us with a new work ethic, one that attempts to resolve the ambivalent relationship between self and organization by drawing upon the Protestant ethic and re-visioning it according to New Age values."

The re-evaluation of Weber's legacy led Casey (2004) to review the extant crisis of bureaucracy, a classical Weber-ian contribution to organizational sociology. Casey documented the incorporation of unconventional, seemingly irrational, practices in organizational routines around the world (Casey, 2004) even when, as originally formulated, bureaucracy had differed from previous organizational forms in its rationalization of authority and power. Linking this bureaucratic crisis to the "wider crisis of modernity," Casey (2004: 65) argued that the challenges being faced by bureaucratic organizations are symptomatic of a wider societal movement away from ennui and meaninglessness in individual lives borne of over-rationalization. Earlier, religion used to provide for an individual's meaning needs. Since then, quite in tune with Weber's predictions, increased modernization and secularization in organizations has led to the individual being reduced to *homo economicus*, a rational benefit maximizing economic entity. Organizational legitimacy being granted to only the rational economic aspects of an individual, coupled with the increasing centrality of organizations in an individual's life, has meant that the meaning-making function of religion are lost sight of leading to a wide-spread sense of ennui. Such a change was presaged by Weber, Casey claims, and argues that Weber had also foreseen the consequent "turn to meaning-seeking and value-reconstruction after the crisis of modernity and its social defragmentation."

2.2.2 M. P. Follett's contributions to SAW

Mary Parker Follett, who wrote in the first quarter of the twentieth century, is another management author who is credited with reflecting spiritual concerns in her writings. She wrote:

> There are leaders who do not appeal to man's complacency but to all their best impulses, their greatest capacities, their deepest desires. I think it was Emerson who told us of those who supply us with new powers out of the recesses of the spirit and urge us to new and unattempted performance. This is far more than imitating your leader. In this conception of Emerson's, what you receive from your leader does not come from him, but from the "recesses of the spirit." Whoever connects me with the hidden springs of all life, whoever increases the sense of life in me, he is my leader. (Metcalf & Urwick, 1941:294)

Quatro (2004) cites contributions from M. P. Follett to find continuity in the academic discourse of which SAW is a branch. In particular, Quatro refers to Follett's contributions to raise the following issues:

Follett had identified management-labor antagonism of interests as the basis for many organizational ills and suggested pushing down responsibility and authority down to individual employees and work-groups levels. This model of organizational integration featured by "collective responsibility" can be seen as the factor essential to the tenets of empowerment and shared governance central to the SAW discourse today.

Quatro acknowledges Follett for having championed the idea of elimination of boundaries leading to joint problem solving and providing for interconnectedness not only within departments but also the firm and its environment. The argument closely mirrors the arguments for Organizational Interweaving and Coordination that feature in many SAW articles.

Follett is also credited with a model of purposeful leadership that advanced the idea of 'power-with' rather than 'power-over' one's employees. Intentional humility and strength of mission and vision are features of this leadership style that appear to have been adopted by the SAW literature.

The "higher purpose" of work and organizational life that has become a central tenet of SAW literature also appears to have been considered by Follett when she suggested that employees would be willing to sacrifice compensation for more task significance, indicating the need for meaningfulness in organizational routines and tasks.

2.2.3 Abraham Maslow

The father of humanistic psychology, Abraham Maslow is best known for his 'Hierarchy of Needs' model. Beginning with physiological and ending with self-actualization, Maslow appears to have become synonymous with the theories of human motivation to the extent that a journal paper is titled *Motivation: That's Maslow. Isn't it?*. While the theory has been criticized on methodological issues from the beginning, its intuitive validity amongst practitioners is beyond debate.

Complete intellectual, emotional and spiritual fulfillment appears at the end of the Hierarchy of Needs model and is related to meaningful work provided by the organization. Similar calls for a higher purpose relating individual work domain with organizational vision and mission remains an important facet of the current SAW discourse.

Arguing for enlightened management, Maslow too emphasized on a management style that sees the other as a means to accelerate one's self-actualization and advance organizational performance (Primeaux & Vega, 2002). The style was a crucial departure from the earlier antagonistic management-employee relationship marked by command and control, wherein management assumed all responsibility for rationality and the employees were to be controlled for executing the decisions. Instead, Maslow (1998:103) saw the organizational goals as shared and insisted that a more democratic managerial style served better, an assertion duly echoed by the SAW advocates:

> ...even the most tough-minded person in the world would have to draw the same conclusion as the most tender-minded in the world from these data, that a certain kind of democratic manager makes more profit for the firm as well as making everybody happier and healthier.

Other than the two central ideas for Maslow that have already been incorporated into SAW discourse, another significant feature of Maslow's later thoughts still remains to be adopted into SAW: the positioning of organized religion in workplace spirituality. Maslow (1998:83) in speaking on "spirituality in management" says:

> Enlightened management is one way of taking religion seriously, profoundly, deeply and earnestly... for those who define religion (and spirituality) in terms of deep concern with the problems of human beings, with the problems of ethics, of the future of man, then this kind of philosophy, translated into the work life, turns out to be very much like the new style of management and of organization.

2.2.4 Robert Greenleaf's Servant Leadership

Greenleaf's servant leadership is yet another scholarly tradition that many SAW scholars utilize in their arguments. Marking a break from the widespread leadership literature that saw a leader as an autonomous autocratic agent directing the employees towards meeting objectives the leader had enunciated, Greenleaf saw the servant-leader as inspirational and service-centered. In Greenleaf's conceptualization, a motivation for service, and not accumulation of power, characterized a servant leader. Quatro (2004) too finds Servant leadership's focus on others' needs, and service to the wider society as themes that are held in common by the current SAW discourse. Russell and Stone (2002:145) elaborate upon this feature of Greenberg's conception of Servant Leadership:

> Optimally, the prime motivation for leadership should be a desire to serve. Servant leadership takes place when leaders assume the position of servant in their relationships with fellow workers. Self-interest should not motivate servant leadership; rather, it should ascend to a higher plane of motivation that focuses on the needs of others.

Citing the above scholars as having presaged SAW, it is argued that SAW scholars ought to pay more heed to their intellectual heritage lest the contemporary organizational spirituality literature be branded as lacking "theoretical context" (Quatro, 2004:229).

Summing up this section, while a dominant theme in SAW literature is that the current upsurge in interest is a spontaneous response to the discontinuous changes in an employee's socio-cultural, economic and professional environment, a rival viewpoint finds scholarly continuity in the major SAW themes. This study argues that the two positions on SAW's emergence - spontaneous expression and historical inheritance – need not necessarily be seen as dichotomous. The two positions could be seen as complementary in nature. While concerns relating to the human element inside organizations have been present in literature since Chester Barnard's contribution in 1930, the current social context renders such issues more salience. It is in this backdrop that the traditional heritage of religion and spirituality is being offered as an appropriate solution for resolving individual and organizational issues.

Drawing upon these, the implication for an empirical enquiry could be to examine if there has indeed been an upsurge in interest in SAW inside organizations and if this rise in interest can be linked to the changed socio-cultural, organizational and personal contexts. Alternatively, the SAW interest may perhaps be taken as an enduring value inside organizations.

For the purposes of this study then, an empirical examination of the antecedent factors that inspired practitioners to take up SAW would further advance the extant SAW literature.

2.3 Central Debates in SAW literature

In the nascent field of Spirituality at Work, the scholarly literature is marked by vigorous debates on a few central issues. Owing to the varied assertions in literature about the applicability of SAW prescriptions to all organizations, the debates hinges on a few issues. These issues include: the perceived similarity between the constructs of religion and spirituality; the contention that the ineffable and subjective nature of spirituality defies attempts at defining it; the argument about whether it is the individuals or the organizations which drive the movement; the linking of the 'traditionally perceived as non-material' spirituality to material outcomes inside organizations; and the disavowal of context in the extant literature of SAW. The debates that have been fundamental to SAW literature are detailed below.

2.3.1 To be identified with religion or not, that's the question: The denied religious underpinnings of SAW

Owing to the tension borne of religion being regarded as divisive inside the workplace even when most individuals' sense of spirituality derives from a religious source, scholars have long debated the place of religion in organizational spirituality. A survey of the SAW literature brought out distinct themes about the place of religion in SAW. While many writers argue for examining religion and spirituality separately in the context of work and organizations, they differ on identifying the roots of this distinction. While there are those who would argue that religion and spirituality are separate even conceptually (Bradley & Kauanui, 2003; Kinjerski & Skrypnek, 2004), others claim that pragmatic considerations force this separation (Forray & Stork, 2002).

Siding with those who claim there are fundamental differences between religion and spirituality, Mitroff and Denton (1999a) claim that their respondents accepted spirituality as a fit topic for organizations while dismissing the use of religion in the workplace. Mitroff and Denton (1999a:23-25) concluded their landmark study on spirituality at work with the following ten elements of organizational spirituality:

♦ Spirituality is not denominational.

♦ Spirituality is broadly inclusive; it embraces everyone.

♦ Spirituality is universal and timeless.

♦ Spirituality is the ultimate source and provider of meaning and purpose in our lives.

♦ Spirituality expresses the awe we feel in the presence of the transcendent.

♦ Spirituality is the sacredness of everything, including the ordinariness of everyday life.

♦ Spirituality is the deep feeling of the interconnectedness of everything.

♦ Spirituality is integrally connected to inner peace and calm.

♦ Spirituality provides one with an inexhaustible source of faith and willpower.

♦ Spirituality and faith are inseparable.

Amongst the ten elements suggested above, the first three can be characterized as *not-religion*, inasmuch as they imply that spirituality is not formal, structured or organized, factors totally opposed to the features of conventional religion. Hicks (2002) perceptively observes that for most scholars, spirituality is defined "by way of the *via negative*". Not-religion is how spirituality is posited to appeal to an increasingly secularized audience. While secularization (the diminishing hold of religion on the modern psyche) is commonly cited as the reason for the unambiguous neglect of religion in the SAW literature, others attribute it to contemporary managerial emphasis on diversity and inclusion (Forray and Stork, 2002). Nevertheless, a dominant section of SAW literature today approves of fundamental separation between the themes of integrative spirituality and divisionary religion.

However, another section of SAW literature argues, "a meaningful conversation about spirituality sans religion is dubious" (Harvey, 2001). It contends that the widespread SAW claim of "spirituality unites, while religion divides" is problematic and ignores serious issues in the practice of research in the field (Hicks, 2002:380). In trying to 'define away' the negatives of exclusive religions, SAW writers have conceptualized spirituality too broadly for it to be coherent [an argument echoed by Benefiel (2003: 383): 'definitions so broad that they lose substance'] and the emphasis on creation of common ground through spirituality has overlooked difficult and divisive issues in its application. Instead, Hicks argues, a framework is required which will enable conflicting views and practices of a diverse workforce to be negotiated within organizations.

In relating the 'not-religion' emphasis in SAW literature with his consulting experience, Harvey (2001:377) observes:

> ...I have found that many major decisions at the highest level of all kinds of organizations are made on the basis of prayer. Furthermore, I find that leaders who wield extraordinary influence in a wide variety of venues are deeply concerned about the spiritual side of their leadership roles, and they are starved for opportunities to discuss it. But when they — real, living leaders — do discuss their spiritual concerns, they mostly do so using words like "God," "Allah," "religion," "prayer," "church," "worship," "Jesus," and "Buddha." Alternatively, they sure as hell do not talk about "work spirit," "Spirit," "organizational transformation," "Open Space," "energy sources," and "organization as community."

Harvey concludes that the SAW writers in choosing to use "euphemistic substitutes" for religion/God in their works have not done justice to the phenomenon they are studying. Harvey advises the SAW scholars to cultivate the fearlessness required to break fresh ground in the domain and maintain their spiritual integrity.

Beyond the argument based on evidence from practicing managers, scholars have also argued against the religion-spirituality distinction pointing out that the two constructs are inherently intertwined (Hill et al., 2000a). Hill et al (2000) go into the literature related to spirituality and argue that the distinction accorded to spirituality owes itself to the rise of secularism and disenchantment with religious institutions in the western society in the latter half of the 20th century. They claim that cultural distancing of spirituality from its roots of religion has led to a more favorable connotation for the former while the latter is considered a hindrance in the path of individual experience of the spiritual. Driven by the schism, spirituality is accorded an individual, experiential character even as religion is supposed to inhere in institutional forms and obscurantist beliefs. However, locating the search for the sacred [sacred being defined as 'a socially influenced perception of either some sense of ultimate reality or truth or some divine being/object' (ibid.:67).] as being central to the two constructs of Religion and Spirituality, this forced distinction is fraught with two main pitfalls.

1. A polarization between the two closely intertwined constructs would deny that all religions are interested in matters spiritual and that every form of religious and spiritual expression occurs in a social context (Zinnbauer et al, 1999). Further, the polarization of religion and spirituality in good/bad camps would deny that each could be manifested in healthy as well as unhealthy ways.

2. The distancing of spiritual from its sacred features, thus denying the irrevocable ultimate reality / divine connotation, would reduce it to either an ideology or a mere lifestyle.

It has been argued that keeping the sacred out of the spiritual divests spirituality of its essence (Zinnbauer et al., 1999). Arguing that the sacred remains central to both religion and spirituality, scholars argue that the definitions of religion and spirituality both are in dire need of empirical grounding and improved operationalization (Hill et al., 2000a).

From the above survey of SAW literature on religion and spirituality, it can be concluded that the dominant section of current SAW research disregards the possibility that religion could enhance the individual predilection towards a spiritual engagement with work. While doubts have recently been raised about this assumed disconnect between religion and spirituality, the dominant section of SAW still views spirituality through a *via negative* lens. Faced with this situation, it could be asked if religion has been left out of the organizational enquiry lens only because of the fears of it being misunderstood in the academic context of a rigid sacred-secular divide. This position appears to be supported by scholars (see Mitroff and Denton, 1999, as an illustrative example) who argue that the North American emphasis on church-state separation has led to the current neglect of religion and spirituality in academic management literature. However, to the extent that religion contributes to meaning provision amongst its adherents, an empirical question could be if it is possible for individuals to strip off their religious identity when entering the workplace. To bow down then before the long accepted separation of the secular and sacred only undermines the possible benefits that the religiously inclined individuals can bring to a workplace that is conducive to the practice of SAW.

In conclusion, it can be argued that while distinguishing between religion and spirituality may be deemed essential to make SAW popular and more widely acceptable, it cannot remain the primary objective of any scholarly enquiry. While Harvey (2001) has argued for the re-incorporation of religion in organizational enquiry, empirical evidence may perhaps strengthen the case against the rigid sacred-secular divide in the organizational context. *An empirical examination of issues relating to religion and spirituality inside organizations would shed some more light on this issue.*

2.3.2 Defining the ineffable: Spirituality at Workplace

Despite the rising popularity of spirituality and its application in the workplace, conceptual ambiguity remains the norm as organizational researchers struggle over the very possibility of defining SAW. To some degree, the organizational literature itself perpetuates ambiguity either by accepting spirituality simply as a mystical or soulful experience (Neal, 1997) or by ignoring its definition altogether. The argument for ignoring a definition bases itself on the universal nature of spirituality to deduce "spirit can't be precisely defined, for in defining we delimit; we form boundaries around that which we are defining to differentiate it" (Gull & Doh, 2004).

Still another reason for lack of definitions is the perceived ineffability of spirituality. Neal (1997) observes that defining spirituality is difficult because people "are trying to objectify and categorize an experience and way of being that is at the core very subjective and beyond categorizing" (p. 123). This position against defining spirituality is further elaborated upon thus: "The rank-ordering and quotient mania is trying to invade an arena, which is simply beyond the bounds of any kind of quantification. Such efforts amount to a brand of reductionism that entails the futility of converting into objective terms what is irrevocably subjective" (Chakraborty, 2004:47). A single comprehensive definition too is deemed difficult owing to "our limited understanding of contemporary religion and spirituality" (Hill et al., 2000b:52). However, scholars also reject the claims about the subjective and ineffable nature of the construct to argue that the concept of organizational spirituality "is not so much elusive and intangible as confused and imprecise" (Brown, 2003).

Furthermore, scholars also agree that well-defined constructs help empirical research and thus if the field has to progress and gain acceptance from the wider academic community, it will have to develop well-defined constructs with their measures and instruments for theory building (Giacalone & Jurkiewicz, 2003b).

It is in that spirit of search for a "scientific" definition that the SAW literature was examined to encounter a broad variety of conceptions. The diversity of definitions is deemed inevitable due to the intensely personal nature of the construct. A characteristic practitioner-oriented defense of 'allowing a thousand definitional flowers to bloom' position is: "...the importance lies not in providing a single definition for the spirituality term, but rather to first understand the differing perspectives and then to encourage employees to practice their own sense of spirituality in the workplace" (Krishnakumar & Neck, 2002:156).

On a related note, (Mohamed, Hassan, & Wisnieski, 2001) claim there are more definitions of spirituality than there are authors/researchers to write about it! A few representative examples of the definitions available are given below to illustrate the definitional diversity in the field today:

> "...spirituality represents a specific form of work feeling that energizes action... In the realm of behavior, spirituality is a subconscious feeling that energizes individual action in relation to a specific task."
> (Dehler & Welsh, 1994:19)

> "...the search for meaning in the ordinary business of everyday life."
> (J. Biberman, Whitty, & Robbins, 1999:251)

> "Being spiritual involves belief and action directed toward aligning oneself with or expression of what is 'sacred'."
> (Bierly II, Kessler, & Christensen, 1999:606)

> "Developing continuity is an exercise in spirituality."
> (Waddock, 1999:332)

> "...the journey toward spirituality represents the quest to unite one's inner and outer world, to provide meaning and purpose to one's life."
> (King & Nicol, 1999:234-235)

> "[spirituality is] about knowing that we're all spiritual beings having a human experience. It's about knowing that every person has within himself or herself a level of truth and integrity, and that we all have our own divine power."
> (Laabs, 1995:64)

"Spirituality need not necessarily involve a belief in some supreme power. Instead, it ought to be redefined in "exclusively human terms."
(Pava, 2003:397)

"...the recognition that employees have an inner life that nourishes and is nourished by meaningful work that takes place in the context of community."
(Ashmos & Duchon, 2000:137)

"...the process of finding meaning and purpose in our lives as well as living out one's set of deeply held personal beliefs."
(Neck & Milliman, 1994)

"Spirituality is an innate and universal search for transcendent meaning in one's life... In addition, although it can be expressed in various ways, we submit that spirituality at work involves some common behavioral components. Above all, it involves a desire to do purposeful work that serves others and to be part of a principled community. It involves a yearning for connectedness and wholeness that can only be manifested when one is allowed to integrate his or her inner life with one's professional role in the service of a greater good... Spiritual elements would include focus on relationships, harmony, balance and meaningful work."
(Ashar & Lane-Maher, 2004:252-253)

Spiritual Management Development programs employ "beliefs in realization of infinite potential, holism (body, mind and soul), and personal and embodied experience."
(Bell & Taylor, 2004)

"Spirit at work is a distinct state that is characterized by physical, affective, cognitive, interpersonal, spiritual, and mystical dimensions. Most individuals describe the experience as including: a *physical* sensation characterized by a positive state of arousal or energy; positive *affect* characterized by a profound feeling of well-being and joy; *cognitive* features involving a sense of being authentic, an awareness of alignment between one's values and beliefs and one's work, and a belief that one is engaged in meaningful work that has a higher purpose; an *interpersonal* dimension characterized by a sense of connection to others and common purpose; a *spiritual* presence characterized by a sense of connection to something larger than self, such as a higher power, the Universe, nature or humanity; and a *mystical* dimension characterized by a sense of perfection, transcendence, living in the moment, and experiences that were awe-inspiring, mysterious, or sacred."
(Kinjerski & Skrypnek, 2004)

"...the basic feeling of being connected with one's complete self, others and the entire universe. If a single word best captures the meaning of spirituality and the vital

role that it plays in people's lives, that word is interconnectedness."
(Mitroff & Denton, 1999a:83)

Earlier reviews of SAW literature have attempted to make sense of this diversity by suggesting categories in which various definitions can be placed. One such classification suggests three categories of SAW definitions: the first defines spirituality in personal terms; the second focuses on the applied aspect of spirituality; and the third looks at the characteristics of the spiritual organization (Schmidt-Wilk, Heaton, & Steingard, 2000). Krishnakumar and Neck (2002) in another classification focus on the origin of such definitions to suggest three perspectives: the intrinsic-origin view, the religious view and the existentialist perspective. The intrinsic-origin view sees spirituality as a concept that originates from the inside of the individual. The religious view closely relates spirituality to the traditional religious bases to remain the most controversial as has been seen in an earlier sub-section. The existentialist view reflects the dominant concern for finding meaning and purpose in the workplace.

Another threefold typology - Religious Spirituality, Secular Spirituality and Mystical Spirituality – can be seen as a way out of the religion-spirituality dilemma for scholars (Gibbons, 2000a). Religious spirituality incorporates the theistic beliefs reflected in ceremonies and rituals within both the sacred spaces of places of worship and the everyday life. Secular Spirituality would include beliefs that could be pantheistic or atheistic but would incorporate earth-centered, nature-centered, and humanistic spiritualities. Its practices would include social and environmental activism. Mystical Spirituality, he argues, would be similar to religious spirituality in their theistic orientation without their ceremonies and ritualistic expression to be reflected both in sacred and routine realms.

This study argues (with Dean et al., 2003) that the extant definitional multiplicity in SAW hinders further development of the field by providing few generalize-able measures. The definitional diversity of SAW needs to be reduced to a few central themes. These themes could then be operationalized into instruments for SAW measurement and thus facilitate further theory building. Feeling the same need, a number of studies have been conducted with this approach and a few themes identified as being central to the study of SAW. Four such studies are summarized below to indicate a conceptual convergence in SAW.

An oft-cited study in this direction finds three themes as being central to SAW: Inner Life, Meaning at work, and Sense of Connection and Community (Ashmos & Duchon, 2000). Ashmos and Duchon conceive of the Inner Life as spiritual identity in Vaill's terms (1998:218): "the feeling individuals have about the fundamental meanings of who they are, what they are doing, and contributions they are making" and argue that for SAW to thrive it is essential for organizations to appreciate that individuals have an inner life that needs encouragement. The meaning at work component meant work that lent meaning and purpose to an employee's life. The third component indicated the trans-individual character of SAW relating to the fellowship aspect of spiritual literature.

Based on Ashmos and Duchon's formulation, another study placed forward Meaningful Work, Sense of Community and Alignment of Values as the central dimensions of SAW where Alignment of Values encompassed the interaction of employees with the larger organizational purpose (Milliman et al., 2003).

Another effort in this direction, based on an inductive reading of SAW literature, placed forward Transcendence of Self, Holism and harmony, and Growth as the three essential dimensions of SAW (Ashforth & Pratt, 2003). A connection to something greater than oneself is what defines transcendence of self; integration of various aspects of oneself into a roughly coherent and consistent self and behavior in accordance with it is implied by the second dimension whereas a sense of self-development in terms of realization of one's aspirations and potential underlies the dimension of Growth.

The most recent such effort argued that a conceptual convergence was emerging in the field of workplace spirituality and proposed that the current SAW literature is converging towards the following four recurring themes: 1. Self-Workplace Integration, 2. Meaning in Work, 3. Transcendence of Self, and 4. Personal Growth and Development of One's Inner Life at Work (Sheep, 2004). Sheep defines his first theme 'Self-Workplace Integration' as "a personal desire to bring one's whole being into the workplace (as workgroup or organization)-specifically, not to check one's spiritual component at the door." The second theme of' Meaning in Work' is taken to imply convergence of meaning in one's life with that of one's work. The third aspect 'Transcendence of Self' is the most complex for Sheep. Attributing the need for transcendence in the workplace context to the increasingly central role that the workplace has assumed in people's life, Sheep admits that what is to be transcended is rather difficult to pin down. He then argues for adopting the conceptualization of "company as community" (Mirvis, 1997:200) for this particular theme. The fourth central theme for Sheep is 'Personal Growth and Development of One's Inner Life at Work.' Placing this Higher Order need in Maslow's hierarchical needs framework allows Sheep to relate it to achieving one's *full potential*.

The present study based itself on these definitional indicators and other extant SAW literature to conclude that three themes may be taken as central to a comprehensive, and yet parsimonious, study of SAW: Integrity/Wholeness, Meaningful Work, and Larger than oneself. The rationale for the choice of these three specific themes, and how the choice improves upon the existing models, is outlined below:

2.3.2.1 Integrity/Wholeness

There is an increasing appreciation of the fact that people bring their whole selves to work – an idea that includes the spiritual self (Dehler & Welsh, 1994). Mitroff and Denton (1999) in their seminal study of spirituality in the workplace argue that until the organizations learn to harness the "whole person" they cannot produce world-class products and services. Placing individuals' need to manifest not only their intellect but also their feelings and emotions and even their spirit in the workplace at the centre of their framework, Mitroff and Denton (1999) claim that "(t)he need to feel whole is integral to spirituality in virtually any setting where people attempt to find meaning."

However, beyond the sense indicated in Mitroff and Denton (1999) in terms of an individual not being forced to leave out a specific aspect of one's personality out of the workplace, Integrity/Wholeness in this framework also incorporates the idea of being able to express all parts of oneself at work. Authenticity - conceived as "an experienced consistency between words and action: in order to be considered authentic – or genuine – rhetoric would seemingly have to align with actions" (Johansson & Örndahl, 2003) - is thus integrated in this model. While the issue of authenticity has been examined in the careers of professionals in creative industries (Svejenova, 2005), it can be argued that the issue would be equally relevant to all those who place an emphasis on leading non-compartmentalized lives. It has also been suggested that practice of authenticity would increase feelings of psychological safety (Edmondson, 1999) induced by the sense of mutual respect in contexts that allow people to be themselves.

Further, this study argues that Sheep's fourth dimension of 'Personal Growth and Development of One's Inner Life at Work' is more appropriately placed within the theme of Integrity/Wholeness. To the extent that the focus in 'Personal Growth and Development of One's Inner Life at Work' is on achieving one's full potential, it is more suitably placed as a component of the Integrity/Wholeness theme.

Integrity/Wholeness in the proposed framework thus encompasses the argument for seeing SAW in terms of valuing an organizational member in one's wholeness and placing an emphasis on individuals leading a non-fragmented life. It is thus argued that Integrity/Wholeness construct proposed in this framework not only covers the domain covered by Ashmos and Duchon's *Inner Life* construct – inasmuch as the Wholeness issue would involve the idea of an Inner Life –but goes beyond it by adding the idea of authentic expression in the workplace. Further, the incorporation of Sheep's theme of *Personal Growth and Development of One's Inner Life at Work* makes the Integrity/Wholeness theme dynamic in nature.

2.3.2.2 Meaningful Work

The other theme most consistently present in most SAW articles is 'Meaningful work' since the central component of SAW literature is indeed the issue of employees' search for meaning in their lives leading them to look for meaning in their workplace as well. The many definitions of spirituality used in relation to work (J. Biberman & Whitty, 1997; Cavanagh, 1999; Emmons, 2005; Kahnweiler & Otte, 1997; Mitroff & Denton, 1999a; Neck & Milliman, 1994) treat spirituality as a meaning-making construct. This question of meaning can take many forms: "What is the meaning of life? What is the meaning of *my* life? What do we live for? What shall we live by? If we must die, if nothing endures, then what sense does anything make?" (Yalom, 1980:419).

It is commonly argued that there is a crisis of meaning at work today and that individuals are not content to view their jobs only in terms of the attendant material benefits but want their jobs to contribute a sense of meaningfulness and purposefulness to their lives. Holding the meaning-making property of spirituality as fundamental to SAW lead Neck and Milliman (1994) to define SAW as "… the process of finding meaning and purpose in our lives as well as living out one's set of deeply held personal beliefs." Ashmos and Duchon (2000:136) too argue for conceptualizing human beings as primarily spiritual who "express inner life needs by seeking meaningful work."

However, despite the centrality of meaning and meaning-making to SAW studies only one study in the SAW domain goes into the concept of meaning *per se*. Lips-Wiersma (2002) looked into psychological literature related to meaning and emerged with three complementary themes: 1. purpose; 2. sense-making; and 3. coherence. The value-driven theme of purpose signifies the reasons for which an individual works and is directed at that which is sought to be realized through one's endeavors. The sense-making aspect of meaning focuses on the process of meaning-making that, even as it draws from past experiences, determines future behavior. Coherence is the integrative framework that binds various elements of one's life into a consistent whole. On first look, it may seem that Lips-Wiersma's theme of coherence overlaps with this study's Integrity/Wholeness theme. However, it can be argued that the aspect of coherence as an integrative framework is better understood as an element of the theme that deals with the issue of wholeness and integration (apropos the integrity and wholeness theme in this study's framework).

In this connection, while a few authors restrict themselves to the meaningful tasks and jobs that a particular organizational position may entail (Duchon & Plowman, 2005) others take it further to the idea of *Calling* (D. T. Hall & Chandler, 2005). The concept of *Calling* indicates a person experiencing work beyond instrumental goal-seeking, beyond a job or career and instead as one that is perceived as one's purpose in life. This study argues that taking one's work as calling would enable individuals to achieve the deepest possible levels of satisfaction and psychological success.

This study's use of the term Meaningful Work then connotes purposeful work that is valued by individuals not just for the associated material outcomes but one that fulfils, even if only in part, the search for meaning and purpose in their lives and helps individuals to take decisions in tune with their purpose.

2.3.2.3. Larger than oneself

The idea that the workplace and its inhabitants need to be factored in into the issue of spirituality at work is intuitively appealing. Not surprisingly, most scholars include this aspect in their formulations in one way or the other. Ashmos and Duchon (2000) include it under the name of *Conditions for community* while Milliman et al. (2003) label it *Community*. Mirvis (1997) speaks about the cornerstones to building community namely, Consciousness of the self, Consciousness of the other, a "Group Consciousness" that is simultaneously aware of the whole *and* the parts, and an alignment with the "unseen order of things". The belonging to a community dimension in Duchon and Plowman's framework (2005) indicates "sharing, mutual obligation and commitment that connect people with each other." While a few authors contend that developing community itself can be seen as an exercise of spirituality (Waddock, 1999), others define spirituality in terms of interconnectedness (Garcia-Zamor, 2003). A few other authors refer to this theme in terms of team-work and a homogenous corporate culture (Ashar & Lane-Maher, 2004) or as the organizational members feeling a sense of interconnectedness with one's complete self, others and the entire universe (Kinjerski & Skrypnek, 2004).

However, it is Sheep (2004) who comes closest to this study's theme of *Larger than oneself* when he labels his third dimension as *Transcendence of self*. Referring to the capacity for self-transcendence, the collective theme that allows the organizational members to connect with their community and share a common identity is termed 'Larger than oneself' in this study. The limits of this expansion of one's identity would depend on the attitude one takes towards it. For the religiously inclined, it could expand one's sense of self to the transcendental, while in "exclusively human terms" (Pava, 2003:397), it would expand to include one's community one feels responsible towards and thus contributes to. It can also be argued that the 'Larger than oneself' element of SAW would necessarily predispose one towards service, a claim made by many SAW theorists without providing this particular argument.

Larger than oneself in the proposed framework thus goes beyond the community dimension as used in other formulations and focuses on the expansion of one's sense of identity. Inasmuch as the emphasis in SAW movement is on the individual transcending one's ego-imposed boundaries and feeling a sense of interconnectedness with others [seen as the essence of SAW by Mitroff and Denton, 1999a], it is imperative that the individual gradually begins to appreciate the sense of a shared identity with the other colleagues at work. Further, the sense of interconnectedness with others would necessarily pre-dispose the individual towards service, long argued to be the "natural expression of spirituality" (Kurth, 2003) but never linked in the manner indicated in this framework.

Empirical validation alone will now confirm if the central features of SAW that have been identified are accepted by practitioners in the field or if these too require further refinement. *It would thus seem that one ought to have a few definitional indicators before initiating research in SAW and then refine it through empirical research. The three definitional indicators of SAW that have been extracted from literature could provide an integrative basis for future SAW studies.*

2.3.3 Who drives the movement?

Beyond the issues relating to SAW's definitions, two themes emerge from the critical argument about who drives the SAW movement and whose benefits ought to be taken as primary in this exercise: the individual's or the organization's.

A section of the literature finds individuals the mainstays of SAW movement, a preference that can be labeled as ***employee-pull***. It cites a growing environmental uncertainty, breakdown of other meaning-providing institutions, a changed employment relationship and decreasing employee morale owing to unreasonable downsizing attempts as responsible for changing employee attitudes towards organizations. Further, it argues that a society dominated by corporations can hardly escape the demands from organizations for meaning provision. In fact, a number of authors assume that individuals today are ready to seek spiritual meaning and purpose in their workplaces. As an illustrative example, Vaill (2000) claims:

> We really should not be so surprised about people's readiness: For the past 60 years, one commentator after another has been noting what an organizational society we have become and how profoundly the nature of organizations affects human character, human development, and human feeling. Is it not natural that we should discover that perhaps the human being's oldest conscious preoccupation-our relation to the gods, the perennial philosophy, and the fear and trembling that accompany these ultimate concerns should now turn out to be on people's minds in organizations?

From the theoretical assertions about individuals demanding spiritual fulfillment and purpose in workplaces, Ashar and Lane-Maher (2004) found empirical evidence that individuals do seek an employment that focuses on relationships, harmony, balance, and meaningful work. Mitroff and Denton (1999a), based on their in-depth interviews with 68 senior managers and executives, documented the spiritual aspirations at work to suggest that American executives do yearn to embrace spirituality at work. In its essence, this perspective documents the unease that organizational members feel in an "un-spirited" workplace and their longing for a workplace that would enable them to see their job as a calling, a vocation where they could bring to work all aspects of their personality. This perspective assumes that organizational individuals today are eager to look beyond the material aspects of their jobs to find spiritual fulfillment in their workplaces.

As a counterpoint to the section that sees individuals as the main driving force in SAW, the *organization*-push perspective credits organizations as being the forerunners in this movement. This position argues that organizations today are faced with a dilemma: while on one hand the economic uncertainty in the environment makes it impossible for them to provide employment guarantees that would receive commitment and loyalty in return, the increasing emphasis on employee knowledge in the expanding knowledge economy renders committed human resource most critical for business success. Faced with the inability to provide employment guarantees while simultaneously needing employee commitment, the prospect of being able to utilize employee dedication towards corporate ideals by invoking imagery of religious allegiance and devotion motivates organizational leadership to invoke and promote SAW. Forray and Stork (2002), comment upon one such annotated account of Jeremy working in a hypothetical SAW-oriented company called Orazone:

> Jeremy's experience conforms in part to what has been described as 'new age corporate spiritualism' (Nadesan, 1999). His experience in the workplace is self-fulfilling and productive, it represents the notion that 'a spiritually therapeutic workplace environment enhances productivity by facilitating employees' commitments to organizational goals, which are seen as the route for individual self-actualization' (Nadesan, 1999: 14). Further, the line between his personal needs and the needs of his organization are blurred; Orazone provides him with a means and an environment for realizing his needs (e.g. belongingness or connection) and for self-actualizing by giving to others. His efforts are directed toward the accomplishment of community (i.e. organizational) goals. There are also elements of what Pratt (2000) describes as an 'ideological fortress'.

It would seem that the two perspectives outlined above – individual-pull and organization-push - are irreconcilable. While the former being individual-centric neglects the organizational context altogether, the other's attention on the organization level would render the individual a mere puppet in the hands of managers. The truth would lie somewhere in between. While it would be too much to expect *all* individuals in *all* organizations to aspire for spiritual fulfillment in their workplaces, it would be equally naïve to assume that *all* organizations would be willing to invest in and facilitate the spiritual growth of their employees.

Considerable research scope then exists to enquire into the hitherto 'assumed' readiness of individuals and organizations for engaging themselves fully in the spirituality at work movement.

2.3.4 To what end? The contested SAW outcomes

Beyond the reasons for SAW being approached inside organizations, the issues relating to the attendant consequences have engaged many organizational scholars. At one end of the spectrum are the theologically inclined scholars who caution about the instrumental purposes to which spirituality is being put to in organizations and remind their colleagues about spirituality's essentially non-materialistic nature. Utilization of sacred emotions in service of material pursuits of corporations draws criticisms from these authors and they ask:

> If spirituality is ultimately about non-materialistic concerns, is it appropriate to focus on the material gains to be reaped by integrating spirituality into organizational life... Is more harm than good done by introducing spirituality to organizations through tying spirituality to material gain?
> (Benefiel, 2003:384)

and

> Spiritual growth is intended to heighten devotion to corporate ideal, by imbuing routine organizational life with a heightened sense of the mystical... Ironically, the effort is often driven by very non-spiritual concerns – the desire to increase profits.
> (Tourish & Pinnington, 2002:165)

However, it is also argued that in corporations new ideas are adopted not for their own sake but because they offer certain outcomes of interest to the organizations or individuals. To that end, a variety of potential outcomes from adoption of SAW that have been forwarded in literature. Ranging from the individual to the corporate to the social, these gains are argued to accrue if only SAW were to be practiced by a larger number of individuals/organizations and lived more intensely. Moreover, in consonance with the two themes of employee-pull and organization-push, divergent opinions on the potential outcomes from SAW can be discerned. Detailed benefits from each of these two positions in literature are provided below before describing the evidence on consequences that has emerged from the few empirical studies in SAW.

2.3.4.1 Benefits from individual-pull

The benefits claimed from the section of literature that forwards *employee-pull* argument lists the following benefits from SAW practice:

- With expanding frontiers of one's consciousness, improved intuition and creativity spiritual upliftment will then leave employees happier and more satisfied, causing them to be more creative (Cash & Gray, 2000)

- less compartmentalized lives (Cavanagh, 1999)

- focus on honesty and integrity would lead to improvement in trust levels (Burack, 1999)

- equanimity and clarity (Duerr, 2004)

- fulfillment of higher-order needs of employees would leave them with improved levels of personal fulfillment and deeper levels of satisfaction and contentment (Kriger & Hanson, 1999)

- "...spirituality provides faith, courage and hope that facilitate wiser decision making and actions." (Bierly II et al., 1999:607)

2.3.4.2 Organization-push benefits

This section of literature advances the prospect of the following benefits from implementing SAW:

- alignment of individual and organizational values would engender a feeling of belonging amongst the employees improving organizational commitment (J. Biberman et al., 1999; Milliman, Ferguson, Trickett, & Condemi, 1999:225);

- alignment of personal and organizational values [would] reduce stresses that usually come about owing to conflict between the two and promote an improved connection with one's work, one's colleagues and one's organization and thus lead to improved organizational performance (Mitroff & Denton, 1999a);

- decrease alienation (Cavanagh & Bandsuch, 2002);

- open and clearer communication (Duerr, 2004); and

- a greater identification with the organization and better interpersonal relationships in the workplace are expected to lead to decreased turnover (Laabs, 1995).

In addition, beyond the individual-centered and organization-specific claims, another section of research finds in SAW the germ of a paradigm change that would convert the cold and uncaring organizations into warm and compassionate workplaces that would eventually transform the society for the better. Scholars here call for a broadening of customary organizational objectives and argue that the coming purpose for organizations may well be human well-being (Aga, 2004) or the spiritual development of all their stakeholders (Neal & Biberman, 2004). This argument may be seen as an attempt to preserve the conceptual "purity" of spirituality by advocating a broader and less materialistic purpose for SAW's incorporation in today's organizations.

However, the varied claims about potential benefits to be derived from an application of SAW also prompt a few cautionary voices. These arguments could be divided into two broad themes: one cautions against the premises on which the potential benefits of SAW are based while the other doubts the managerial dedication to the SAW philosophy.

The first cautionary note doubts the validity of SAW's premises. One of the common SAW premise is that workplace has become the most significant source of meaning with the breakdown of other communities in one's life. Bell and Taylor (2003: 337) argue that such a position denies the role of non-work communities in achieving spiritual growth and may eventually lead to totalitarian organizations that have complete control over the lives of their employees.

Another unstated assumption in SAW literature appears to be the harmony of social, organizational, and individual goals. It would help if the researchers were more skeptical of such claims, Forray and Stork (2002) caution the readers as they provide a hypothetical account of a SAW oriented corporation providing for the meaning and community needs of its members even as it was engaged in terrorist operations. Beyond the assumed harmony between social and organizational goals in organizations pursuing the SAW ideology, the unquestioned acceptance of the assumption that individual-organizational interests and goals are in total harmony too betrays the naïve optimism in the SAW discourse. The *employee-pull* argument expects the organization to fall in line with employee aspirations, while the *organization-push* literature assumes that the individuals would be willing to go along with the organizational imperative of incorporating SAW to enhance employee commitment and raise productivity levels.

Other than questioning the assumption of harmony between social, organizational, and individual goals, scholars also warn that the concept has much potential for abuse. Tourish and Pinnington (2002:165) argue, "Promoting spirituality in the workplace is to declare that those who dissent from the ideology do not belong…" and claim that to the extent that SAW discourse cherishes devotion to the corporate ideal it could blur the distinction between personal and public space to promote corporate cultism.

Having detailed the theoretical arguments of potential benefits at employee and organization level along with the cautionary notes that accompanied such claims, a scrutiny of the SAW literature illustrates the contention that scholarly work addressing SAW is only now beginning to move from a conceptual phase to a theory-building-empirical testing phase (Duchon & Plowman, 2005). Very few empirical studies have tried to validate the assertions about potential utility of SAW to service organizational and individual concerns. A summary of the various empirical SAW studies that have been carried out is provided below.

A doctoral study attempted to relate individual, group and organizational levels of workplace spirituality with firm profitability growth rates (Quatro, 2002). Yet another study investigated working executives to relate various levels of workplace spirituality to organizational commitment, intention to quit, intrinsic work satisfaction, job involvement, and organization based self-esteem (OBSE) (Milliman et al., 2003). A recent study utilized Ashmos and

Duchon's survey instrument to a healthcare organization's indicators of performance at work-unit level: 1. Quality (patients' evaluation of overall quality of care); and 2. Sensitivity (patients' evaluation of overall sensitivity of staff providing the care) (Duchon & Plowman, 2005).

Milliman et al. (2003) found that the individual workplace spirituality related positively with organizational commitment; the experience of community at work and alignment of personal- and organizational-values related negatively with intention to quit; experience of meaning and purpose in one's work and community at work was found to have a positive relationship with intrinsic work satisfaction; perceptions of meaningful work and sense of community increased job involvement and heightened OBSE.

Duchon and Plowman (2005) found that at the work-unit level of analysis top three performing units had higher spirituality scores than the bottom three performing units with the exception of the Inner Life component of spirituality. This is the first study to demonstrate that differences in spiritual climates at different work-units could explain differences in performance.

From the evidence presented in this section, it can be concluded that the contested SAW outcomes raise concerns about validating the premises on which SAW claims are based, in particular the readiness of individuals and organizations to practice SAW. Further, though the few studies quoted above have broadly examined the consequences related to SAW inside organizations, no systematic study has examined the consequences of SAW in conceptually distinct organizations. It is towards the establishing the need for examining conceptually distinct organizations in SAW that attention is next directed.

2.3.5 Disavowal of the context

In addition to the various issues with SAW that have been discussed earlier, the locus of SAW has been the subject of considerable debate in literature. The basic issue this debate addresses is if all organizational settings are consistent with the pursuit of spiritual strivings and if all individuals would benefit from the practice of SAW.

A significant criticism of the SAW domain maintains that the discourse de-contextualizes the individual, ignoring the powerful impact of the cultural, organizational and structural conditions in which the person operates. Basing itself on "human capacity for transcendence beyond experience of the physical world" (Bell & Taylor, 2004) the corporation is absolved of all responsibility and the individual is left to seek meaning and purpose by and within oneself. An analysis of spiritual management development programs offered by a number of organizations led Bell and Taylor to conclude that these courses preclude all structural explanations for the contradictory demands being faced by the employee. Consequently, the entire responsibility of bringing about a change – both individual and corporate – is brought to bear on the autonomous individual neutralizing the role of the context in the entire exercise of Spirituality at work.

However, it can be suggested that though spirituality may be deemed an internal aspiration inspiring the individual to search for and move towards integrity and wholeness, meaning and purpose, and develop a larger than oneself identity, all this cannot be pursued in isolation. The context continues to remain important in this endeavor as the internal aspiration is encased in an organizational framework.

In a recent contribution, Porter and McLaughin (2006) cited the various arguments that have been made – in academic articles from 1990 to 2005 - to include the organizational context as a factor influencing leaders' behavior and effectiveness. The authors conducted a literature review of 16-year literature on leadership to examine if the call had been heeded. Porter and McLaughin concluded that in spite of the professed importance of considering the context more number of conceptual than empirical articles deal with the organizational context. Consequently, the field of scholarship by failing to take into account the effect of context on group and individual behavior falls prey to the common criticism that "that much organizational behavior research is irrelevant to the well-being of organizations and their members" (Mowday & Sutton, 1993). In a similar vein, it can be argued that contextual factors would need to be factored in into a study on SAW for it to prove meaningful and relevant.

In general, there can be three strong arguments in favor of considering the context: 1. to appreciate better the person x situation interactions; 2. to make the research literature more interesting and thereby gain the attention of and respect from practicing managers; and 3. to exploit the potential of the context to explain anomalous organizational phenomenon (Johns, 2001).

After examining the importance of the context for an exploration of SAW, attention is now shifted to consider the suitability of all organizational contexts for this purpose. However, SAW literature is sharply divided over this issue: while there are scholars who assert that "work organizations are not readily compatible with spiritual strivings" (Ashforth & Pratt, 2003), others argue equally emphatically that all human organizations are "inherently spiritual places" (P. B. Vaill, 1998).

Two strategies that tackle this issue head-on are presented below. Firstly, an argument in favor of utilizing the mainstream organizational behavior perspective of person-organization fit is claimed to illuminate this debate. Then a specific consideration of the nature of the organization is postulated to impact on the SAW practice.

2.3.5.1 SAW: The question of individual-organization fit

With most articles focused on either the individual desires for expressing spirituality at work or the environmental forces on organizations forcing them to incorporate spirituality in the workplace to ensure commitment and boost satisfaction levels, the issue of individual-organization fit has remained under-examined in the SAW literature (For the introductory contribution to this end, see Sheep, 2004). Indeed, Jurkiewicz and Giacalone (2004: 137) observe that "…while research appears to support the ameliorative impact of workplace spirituality, we must caution that little is known about the interactive effects of personal and workplace spirituality."

It is in this contest that this study proposes the utilization of the Person-Organization (P-O) fit literature from OB – concerning the interaction of both person and situation factors to predict behavior – to study SAW (see Kristof, 1996; Westerman & Cyr, 2004 for integrative reviews of P-O fit literature). Therefore, another promising research area in SAW appears to be the issues related to individual perceptions of desire to express spirituality at work and corresponding conditions provided by the organization.

This study argues that individual perceptions of P-O fit between personal preferences for each of the various dimensions of spirituality at work and the corresponding organizational supply of conditions to facilitate or fulfill those preferences is likely to explain a number of consequences that the SAW literature holds out viz., organizational commitment and job satisfaction. A study of individual perceptions of P-O fit, inasmuch as it relates to the individual desire for spirituality and the facilitating conditions provided by the organization may yield a more refined understanding of SAW's applicability to different organizations.

2.3.5.2 SAW: A panacea for all organizations?

Another significant issue with implications for an empirical enquiry appears to be the uncritical acceptance of the claim that the application of SAW would act as a panacea for all organizational ills. The organizational contexts remain inconsequential to such assertions and the same benefits are assumed to accrue to all organizations. However, the contingency framework of organizational analysis argues that dissimilar demands from organizations operating in different domains would necessitate differential applicability of any concept, leading to diverse outcomes and cautions us against a homogeneous treatment of organizations (see Donaldson, 2001 for a summary of the research area). Thus, with the extant SAW literature being silent on the importance of sectoral differences, another potential area for research could be the applicability of the SAW framework for organizations that provide varying support for the practice of SAW. The first such study that obliquely examined the impact of differential contexts too validated the relevance of the context for invocation and utilization of SAW (Duchon & Plowman, 2005).

An empirical examination focusing on inter-organizational differences would thus help test the hypothesis if organizations with a spiritual mission provide a more conducive environment for spiritually oriented individuals to succeed and flourish. Such an enquiry will also be able to test out a tacit assumption in literature that spiritual elements need to be integrated in organizational structure and processes to facilitate the expression of spirituality at work. For, it makes sense that only if organizations claiming to operate on spiritual principles and moving towards spiritual ends can realize the benefits being held out for ordinary organizations will the other "non-spiritual" organizations be prompted to incorporate similar principles and processes in their own operations.

Uncritical acceptance of SAW outcomes' claims for all organizations merits an examination
of SAW consequences in a variety of organizations to evaluate if dissimilar organizational
contexts lead to differential outcomes.

2.3.6 The issue of SAW manifestation and expression

Yet another issue that has been largely ignored in empirical SAW research is how spirituality could be manifested in an organizational context. The existing SAW studies have broadly examined two specific areas of concern: 1. a conceptualization and testing of SAW construct and its components; and 2. relationship between SAW and individual as well as organizational outcomes. An empirically rigorous examination of how individual and organizational SAW aspirations are manifested into valuable outcomes has however been lacking in the area.

A few studies that have tangentially looked at the issue accept spirituality's inherent personal nature and list the individual qualities that are indicative of SAW practice. A secondary data review of 150 studies argued for a largely individual expression of SAW (Reave, 2005). For Reave, spirituality expresses itself "not so much in words or preaching, but in the embodiment of spiritual values such as integrity, and in the demonstration of spiritual behavior such as expressing caring and concern." Reave claimed that focusing on spirituality may give leadership scholars one way to integrate character, behavior, effect on followers and achievement of group goals. Reave's review focused on traditional spiritual values and isolated certain individual values like integrity, honesty, and humility as the key elements of leaders' success but did not go beyond the individual factors that may influence the practice of SAW.

A theoretical review that investigated the organizational influence on practice of spirituality, while concluding that organizations were essentially incompatible with spiritual strivings, suggested three positions on which organizations could be placed on a continuum in terms of their approach to spirituality (Ashforth & Pratt, 2003). At one end of the continuum could be placed bottom-up employee empowerment oriented organizations where management held an indulgent attitude towards individual spiritual concerns [Enabling organizations]. At the other end of the continuum would be the organizations that prescribed top-down homogenization through a well-defined cosmology [Directing organizations]. In between the two extremes, Ashforth and Pratt also identified a middle-way where the control was mutual and where the issue of spirituality was allowed to co-evolve between the organization and its employees [Partnering organizations]. For each of the three types of organizations, the authors highlighted the distinct ways in which spirituality could be approached at work. Enabling organizations acknowledge individual spiritual strivings and facilitate individual aspirations through prayer groups, yoga, meditation and other spiritual practices. Individual idiosyncrasies in spiritual matters are recognized and respected. Opportunities to engage in spiritual issues are provided to those who may feel the need inside the workplace.

At the other end of the continuum, the Directing organization is characterized by a well-defined and articulated cosmology. That settled cosmology determines the organization's mission, vision, activities, decisions, and even the spiritual practices that the organizational members may engage in. Internalization of organizational cosmology could be encouraged through three levers: 1. recruitment emphasizing P-O fit over technical expertise; 2. pre-determined socialization of individuals through cyclical sense-breaking and sense-giving; and 3. continuous ongoing normative control.

The Partnering organizations, Ashforth and Pratt argue, sought to combine the features of the two extremes and incorporated some personalization from Enabling organizations and a sense of spiritual community from Directing organizations.

The largely uniform treatment of organizations in SAW domain calls for an empirical examination of varied organizational contexts to explore if the issue of manifestation and expression of spirituality differs from one kind of organization to another. It would also help if features that support and facilitate SAW in organizational settings could be isolated and contrasted against those that hinder the practice of SAW.

2.4 Conclusion

The field of SAW has generated considerable interest amongst practitioners and scholars. Being forwarded as a new powerful tool to counter individual alienation in organizations – one that promotes individual fulfillment while enhancing organizational effectiveness and productivity – the literature still features many unresolved research issues.

The issue of why SAW is being seen as having the potential to solve many an organizational ill today merits an examination of the antecedents of this widespread interest. An enquiry into the rationale for SAW's adoption shall also help clarify if indeed conscious moves are being made in this direction or if it is being approached only as another fad. A related claim that calls for empirical validation is the hitherto assumed readiness of individuals and organizations for engaging themselves fully in the spirituality at work movement.

Definitional multiplicity in literature today needs empirical support for capturing essential themes of SAW. This study has identified three elements of this definitional convergence – Integrity/Wholeness, Meaningful work, and Larger than oneself – as being central to an understanding of SAW but these will need to be validated with empirical evidence.

In addition, SAW has been advanced as a panacea for all organizations with its benefits accruing at all possible levels: individual, team level, organizational and social. The scholarly SAW-as-a-panacea claims disregard the possibility that work-demands could differ from one organization to the other. Empirical examination of individual SAW needs and the perceived organizational SAW supplies would help test the validity of uncritical assertion of SAW benefits for all organizations. Further, the utilization of P-O fit lens would help test the interaction effects of individual and the organization on the practice of SAW. Paucity of empirical articles in the literature reviewed points to lack of evidence to support the consequences claims made in various articles. There appears to an urgent need for validating these claims in varying organizational contexts to corroborate the contention of a universal need for meaning and purpose in the workplace.

In the following chapter, these various strands of SAW literature would be brought together to present a conceptual framework that would enable a more robust study of this novel phenomenon in the workplace.

Chapter 3: Conceptual Framework

The previous two chapters have documented the growing interest in SAW and identified some of the reasons why spirituality is being seen as one of the cures for various issues that individuals and organizations are struggling with in the turbulent organizational environment today. The review of literature identified a number of issues and problems with the current state of SAW research and raised a number of questions that need to be examined empirically if spirituality is to be approached in an organizational context.

The present study makes an attempt at dealing with outstanding issues that have been identified in the review of literature earlier and bringing some conceptual and empirical clarity to the issue so that further movement can be made in the understanding of SAW. To that end, this chapter brings together the various issues identified from a critical review of literature from the previous chapter to lead to a conceptual framework that guided the present study.

3.1 SAW definition

A central issue in dealing with the issue of spirituality at work is that there is not enough conceptual clarity about the construct. SAW studies have examined such diverse phenomena under this rubric as utilization of Reiki and Feng-shui in organizations to individuals finding meaning and purpose at work. This eclecticism in SAW studies is apparently endorsed by scholars who argue that given its personal and subjective nature SAW studies shall need to accommodate various conceptions of the construct. Consequently, a clear and precise definition of SAW is argued to be difficult to arrive at. However, regardless of the difficulty in defining the construct, an argument about the potential utility of a concept inside organizations needs to be backed up by a defensible definition. This study argues that spirituality at work confounds scholars primarily in two major ways: 1. the difficulty of pinning down SAW to a single definition; and 2. the assumed dichotomy between religion and spirituality. These two issues will be examined in the sections below to draw implications for this study.

3.1.1 Defining the ineffable

The issue of defining spirituality comes across as a major stumbling block in the empirical examination of issues relating to spirituality at work. While there are those who argue that the essential subjectivity of the construct renders a single correct definition impossible (Gull & Doh, 2004), Brown (2003) argues that the concept of organizational spirituality "is not so much elusive and intangible as confused and imprecise." Further, a section of scholars argue that not defining SAW makes it impossible to compare the findings from different studies (Giacalone & Jurkiewicz, 2003b), a step necessary for theoretical advancement. In between these two diametrically opposite perspectives, a central position is indicated with the suggestion for identification of a few central themes from literature as a starting point and then building it up with inputs from empirical enquiry (Dean, 2004; Dean et al., 2003). Hill et al. (2000: 57-58) too suggest that spirituality should be taken as a multi-dimensional construct (a position supported by Milliman et al., 2003) and recommend a profile analysis of each element individually - and all elements collectively - as a fruitful way of studying the phenomenon.

The literature review chapter identified a three-theme model to conceptualize spirituality at work. It was argued that a conceptual convergence can be discerned in the understanding of spirituality at work with Integrity/Wholeness, Meaningful work, and Larger than oneself as the central themes for approaching spirituality in a workplace context.

It was decided to use these three themes to develop an instrument for collecting data on SAW at individual needs and organizational supplies levels. Other than validating the acceptance of these themes from empirical data other themes relating to SAW were identified through structured interviews with all respondents. Additional details about the precise methodology used for the purpose shall be provided in the next chapter.

The major obstacle in defining SAW in literature having been dealt with, attention is now focused on the next major concern that scholars have in approaching spirituality in a workplace context.

3.1.2 Religion and Spirituality

Another tangible issue that emerges from the debates on defining SAW is its relationship with the contentious issue of religion inside organizations. Religion appears to have been crowded out of organizational studies owing to the separation of the church and the state (Mitroff & Denton, 1999a). Not only has potentially divisive religion lost its earlier hold on individuals, religion as an institution too inspires less confidence today (Cavanagh, 1999). It has also been argued that issues relating to fears of conversion and invasion of privacy have kept scholars away from exploring religion in organizational enquiry (Reave, 2005) leading to a dichotomous relationship between "bad religion" and "good spirituality". Hence, in keeping with the accepted distinction between religion and spirituality, most scholars define SAW primarily as not-religion.

However, the not-religion conceptualization of spirituality does not do justice to SAW's content and spirit (Harvey, 2001). Other arguments have also been made against the religion-spirituality distinction. Scholars claim that the two constructs are inherently intertwined (Hill et al., 2000a) and that keeping the sacred out of the spiritual divests spirituality of its essence (Zinnbauer et al., 1999). Arguing that the sacred remains central to both religion and spirituality, it is argued that the definitions of religion and spirituality both are in dire need of empirical grounding and improved operationalization (Hill et al., 2000a). In this study, an attempt was made to illuminate this debate with inputs from empirical data. Respondents were asked specific questions about their perceptions about spirituality and religion and if the two issues could be separated as suggested by a majority of SAW scholars. Alternatively, they were asked about their suggestions for approaching spirituality inside organizations.

3.2 The forgotten antecedents of SAW

While the SAW literature speaks eloquently about the perceived environmental changes that has led many individuals to take to SAW, there is no empirical validation of this claim. From the review of SAW articles, three broad domains that encourage individuals to take to SAW were apparent: Socio-cultural, Organizational, and Personal.

Amongst the many socio-cultural factors that claim to have been instrumental in leading organizations and individuals to SAW are: improvement in technologies and communication channels increasing exposure to alternative lifestyles, increasing leisure times, and the society itself moving higher on Maslow's hierarchy of needs.

The organizational factors that lead organizations to take up SAW as a management strategy are the challenge to maintain high organizational commitment and satisfaction levels inside organizations even as the earlier psychological contracts that ensured loyalty are being violated in a dynamic business environment that prompts radical measures such as downsizing, restructuring, lay-offs, etc. The resultant increased uncertainty, ambiguity, and insecurity in the workplace (Kolodinsky et al., 2003) is sought to be countered by adopting SAW as a strategy that would heighten devotion to the corporate ideal (Tourish & Pinnington, 2002).

At the personal level of explanations, decline in traditional opportunities for community (Vaill, 1998) that has led individuals to search for meaning and purpose in one's workplace is posited as being the most urgent. It is argued that an exposure to new age philosophies and eastern religions with their emphasis on sanctifying the secular and thus a deeper engagement with one's work has led those in the West to engage with spirituality at work.

3.3 The issue of SAW's manifestation

While there have been varied assertions about the potential utility of SAW for organizations and recommendations on how it could be achieved, there have not been many empirical studies that explicitly study how spirituality is manifested in an organizational context. Duerr (2004) looked at the utilization of contemplative practices inside organizations to conclude that they had a positive effect, both at the individual and organizational levels. However, whether the issue of spirituality goes beyond the contemplative practices alone and whether it can influence regular work-practices too has not yet been examined in literature. Correspondingly, evidence on how organizations can facilitate or hinder the practice of spirituality at work is hard to come by in literature.

To understand the role that organizations can play in realizing the promises of spirituality at work two specific aspects need to be looked into: 1. the extent to which individuals have the autonomy to engage in SAW, and 2. the extent to which the organizations engage in practices that facilitate or hinder the spiritual quest inside the workplace.

This was taken up with the premise that the currently spirit-unfriendly workplaces (Duchon & Plowman, 2005) may be persuaded to take up SAW seriously when the recommendations for facilitating the practice of SAW are backed up by concrete evidence of work-practices from other organizations.

3.4 The under-examined consequences of SAW

That the consequences of SAW too have remained under-examined may be attributed to the widespread belief that spirituality is so ineffable and personal in nature that it is immeasurable. Consequently, most of the SAW articles illustrate the argument that scholarly work addressing SAW is only now beginning to move from a conceptual phase to a theory-building-empirical testing phase (Duchon & Plowman, 2005). The literature review chapter has outlined the meager number of empirical studies in SAW and the issues that have been examined in them.

Faced with the evidence that spirituality is primarily conceptualized in individual terms (Ashmos & Duchon, 2000), it was decided that the appropriate outcome measures would need to be at the individual level. Hence, the outcome measures adopted by Quatro (2002) at the organizational level that included Annualized Average Growth Rate in Total Revenues (TRG), Annualized Average Growth Rate in Net Income (NIG), and Average Return on Assets (ROA) would not really have been germane to this study. Further, the organization-specific outcome measures as adopted by Duchon and Plowman (2005) too would not have allowed inter-organization comparison that was the focus of this study. Hence, the search for appropriate outcome measures was restricted to those at the individual level. In this context, job satisfaction and organizational commitment emerged as natural choices as higher satisfaction and commitment levels are the ordinarily accepted outcomes of SAW practice inside organizations (J. Biberman et al., 1999; Duerr, 2004; Milliman et al., 1999). Hence, Job Satisfaction and Organizational Commitment were selected as the consequences to be tested in this study.

3.4.1 Job satisfaction

The most frequently researched variable in organizational behavior research (Spector, 1997), job satisfaction is an attitudinal variable broadly indicating the degree to which individuals like their jobs. It is amongst the most important areas of concern in organizational behavior research because of its influence on employee behavior and job performance (Wright & Hamilton, 1978). Many employee outcomes have been related to job satisfaction in past studies: job performance, organizational citizenship behavior, withdrawal behavior including absence and turnover, burnout, physical health and psychological well-being, life satisfaction, and counterproductive behavior (Spector, 1997). Issues relating to measurement of job satisfaction and the choice of a specific job satisfaction scale shall be dealt with in the next chapter.

3.4.2 Organizational commitment

The other construct that is argued to lie at the core of organizational psychology – other than job satisfaction - is organizational commitment (Jex, 2002). Broadly, organizational commitment is "the extent to which employees are dedicated to their employing organization and are willing to work on its behalf, and the likelihood that they will maintain membership" (Jex, 2002). Organizational commitment has been linked to a variety of variables that are of interest to researchers and practitioners of management viz., employee retention, attendance at work, in-role job performance, citizenship behavior at work, and employee well-being (Meyer & Allen, 1997). Issues relating to measurement of organizational commitment, its multi-faceted nature and utilization of established organizational commitment scales shall be examined in the next chapter on methodology adopted for this study.

3.5 Disavowal of the context

Beyond the various issues with investigating SAW that have been discussed in the previous sections, perhaps the most significant lacuna in SAW research remains that of disavowal of the context. The basic concern in this issue, as detailed in the literature review chapter earlier, is if all organizational settings are consistent with the pursuit of spiritual strivings. The necessity of considering the context while investigating SAW was elaborated in the previous chapter where an argument was made for a two-pronged strategy to deal with it: 1. utilizing the P-O fit lens to SAW, and 2. considering the organizational context while examining SAW. A detailed treatment of these two strategies is provided below along with an attempt to draw implications for an empirical enquiry.

3.5.1 The Issue of P-O fit in SAW

In a recent article, Jurkiewicz and Giacalone (2004: 137) observe:

> ...while research appears to support the ameliorative impact of workplace spirituality, we must caution that little is known about the interactive effects of personal and workplace spirituality. For example, might a very non-spiritual person have decreased personal performance in a spiritual environment because of the inconsistency between it and her own worldview? Similarly, might a highly spiritual individual in a moderately spiritual environment experience decreases in personal performance because the culture "is not spiritual enough." The likelihood of interactive effects is intriguing and will require a great deal of research to understand.

Person-organization fit – broadly defined as the compatibility between the person and the organization - has been explored in organizational behavior literature for a long time now. Of the many P-O fit conceptualizations that have been offered, one of the accepted ones is the complementary relationship between the perceived needs of the individual and the perceived supplies provided by the organization (Kristof, 1996). It should be possible to measure the P-O fit in SAW terms by assessing the individuals' preferences for SAW and individual perception of organizational SAW supplies on the three central themes of SAW that have been identified to assess the hitherto disregarded P-O interaction effects. The first step in this direction is recorded in the form of an Academy of Management 2004 Meeting paper where Sheep (2004) argued for P-O fit as a mainstream theoretical context for the operationalization and measurement of workplace spirituality. Sheep linked P-O fit on four SAW themes to various organizational outcomes. However, in this study it was considered necessary to focus on the three central themes that capture SAW issues better as indicated in the earlier section on SAW definition and thus contribute to further theory-building in SAW.

3.5.2 Does the organizational context matter?

Beyond the individual's fit with the organization, there also exists the contingency perspective from which the disavowal of context can be approached. The contingency framework of organizations (Donaldson, 2001) cautions us against the assumed homogeneity of organizations and advises comparison of organizations from dissimilar contexts before advocating uniform recommendations. Similar concerns are also visible in SAW literature: "At present, the literature on spirituality in organizations does not assist us in understanding how spirituality is experienced by individuals in different kinds of organizations, or how organizations either explicitly use or deny the existence of spirituality" (Boyle & Healy, 2003).

Since spirituality is claimed to be a dynamic process interconnected with all types and levels of experience – social and situational, as well as personal (Zinnbauer et al., 1999) - it can be argued that the context would exert a significant influence by either enabling or constraining the practice of spirituality inside organizations. It can thus be inferred that spirituality's behavioral expression would be influenced by the nature of the workplace. It is in this context that reference can be made to extant SAW studies from various contexts.

In a wide-ranging study of spirituality in corporate America, apprehensions about one's spiritual identity being exploited left most respondents hesitant to raise and discuss spiritual concerns and issues in the workplace (Mitroff & Denton, 1999a). Partly, the inability to address SAW in corporate contexts was also reflected in the poor response rate that the researchers received. The researchers argued that the deep seated ambivalence about spirituality inside corporations was reflected in the form of frequently played game of "you go first." While the employees would expect their supervisors to make the first move in this direction, the supervisors maintained that they themselves would have no objections if their employees brought out spiritual issues in the open. The game resulted in the spiritual issues not being raised at all.

Another study examined the issue of employees' hesitation in expressing their spirituality in the workplace context (M. Lips-Wiersma, 2002). Her findings echo Mitroff and Denton (1999) in that her respondents too felt that spirituality comprised deeply held values too close to one's sense of identity and thus was a topic that was too risky to voice in the workplace.

Consequently, individuals self-censured their expression of spiritual values, beliefs, and attitudes. Expression of spirituality was withheld due to the apprehension of offending one's peers who may not share those values. Lips-Wiersma (2002) argued that the typical organization's focus on mastery – with the independent and autonomous person being rewarded for distinctive efforts – militates against the basic level of intimacy that is required to express one's spirituality in the workplace. Individuals inside a mainstream workplace thus grapple with the tensions of the need to belong against the need to express their spirituality. Lips-Wiersma (2002) concluded that such a strain could lead to spirituality being perceived as a source of marginalization in the workplace.

Based on the not too encouraging findings about the prospect of expression of spirituality inside a mainstream workplace, it can be argued that before SAW can be studied in corporate organizations – where over a period of time it may become less of a taboo subject to discuss - scholars may need to look for organizations that offer a more conducive environment for the practice of spirituality. It is in the search for more conducive environments for SAW practice that a particular classification of organizations proved useful (Etzioni, 1964). Etzioni's classification proposes a typology comprising three types of organizations: "Coercive" organizations, such as asylums and prisons, that use coercive mechanisms like physical confinement and threats; "Utilitarian" organizations, such as businesses and bureaucracies, which utilize calculative control mechanisms like material rewards; and "Normative" organizations, such as social work and religious organizations that utilize identification-based involvement with symbolic rewards or acceptance.

Organizational scholars, it has been argued (Lois, 1999), have grappled with issues with evidence derived primarily from research on utilitarian organizations, such as corporations, or on settings such as business schools that prepare their inmates for corporate careers. Coercive organizations like prisons and psychiatric facilities have drawn lesser attention from organizational scholars to the extent that these organizations remain underrepresented in organizational literature (earlier examples from the genre are Goffman, 1961; Irwin, 1970). Normative organizations – with very few exceptions (Kanter, 1968; Simons & Ingram, 1997) - have been incorporated into organizational literature even less frequently, and thus remain the most underrepresented of Etzioni's organizational types.

Relating this discussion to empirical SAW studies, diverse contexts like Southwest Airlines (Milliman et al., 1999), academic institutions (Bradley & Kauanui, 2003), nursing institutions and hospitals (Duchon & Plowman, 2005; Grant, 2004), the army (Fry, Vitucci, & Cedillo, 2005) and a sampling of Fortune 500 companies (Quatro, 2002) have been explored in examining SAW. Occupational background has been proposed as a potential contributor to group differences between the clergy and nurses on their policies of spirituality and religiousness (Zinnbauer et al., 1999) but an empirical examination of conceptually dissimilar contexts and their implications for SAW has not been attempted so far.

It can be concluded therefore that SAW literature available today does little justice in representing organizations that could answer to the prescriptive model held out for SAW practice. This study argues that as against the mixed evidence on SAW available from the mainstream commercial organizations the non-profit sector may be a more promising avenue to explore SAW issues. Thus, this study argues that it is in the non-profit organizations that discussions on SAW could be more easily accessed as against the presently available ambivalent evidence from the corporate sector. Before listing the specific features that make the non-profits more suitable for exploring SAW, a brief outline of their central characteristics is provided below.

Even as the boundaries of the non-profit sector remain contested (P. D. Hall & Burke, 2002), scholars have attempted to provide a few defining characteristics. For instance, a seminal study of the non-profit sector identified three basic characteristics of the organizations it encompasses: 1. a non-coercive participation model; 2. non-distribution of surplus amongst stakeholders; and 3. their featuring ambiguous ownership and accountability relationships (Frumkin, 2002:3). Yet another study identified five important characteristics of the non-profit organizations: 1. Formal – an organizational form or system of operation that is institutionalized to a certain extent; 2. Private – institutional distinction from the government; 3. Nonprofit distributing – profits generated being plowed back to serve the basic mission of the organization; 4. Self-governing; and 5. Voluntary – a more dominant utilization of volunteers for the achievement of organizational aims (Schepers et al., 2005).

In particular, the suitability of the non-profit sector for SAW research is argued based on certain interesting parallels between SAW recommendations and corresponding features of the sector. It can be demonstrated that the recommendations of SAW scholars for improving the workplace environment to help initiate and advance the practice of SAW are prominent features of the non-profit organizational framework. This position is argued because of the following distinctive characteristics of non-profits that correlate well with the SAW scholars' recommendations:

1. "...for many, nonprofit and volunteer work is attractive because it represents a way to connect work activity to core beliefs" (Frumkin, 2002:96), which has been one of the central arguments for employees becoming interested in SAW.

2. "...nonprofits, particularly faith-based nonprofits, were in a position to bring to social programs something that public entitlements had long lacked – namely, a moral or *spiritual component*" (Frumkin, 2002:18), a feature intrinsically connected to the SAW domain.

3. "Volunteers work(ing) of their own volition" (Frumkin, 2002:3), a non-profit feature that can be closely related to employees taking up those activities which gives their lives meaning and purpose. It can also be related to the concept of *calling* that had been identified as a derivative of the Meaningful work component of SAW definition.

4. Non-profits' "conscious disavowal of commercial markets" (Frumkin, 2002:9) too closely mirrors the beyond-profit refrain of SAW literature.

5. "...simultaneous support (for) the autonomy of the private individual actor while affirming the importance of shared and public purposes" (Frumkin, 2002:19). Spiritual Management Development programs, it has been mentioned, are characterized by the stress that is placed on autonomy for their participants even as the feeling of community with other organizational participants is emphasized.

6. Non-profits create value that may be entirely psychic and arise "simply from the act of expressing commitment, caring, and belief" (Frumkin, 2002:23). This particular feature may be linked to the aspiration for non-material benefits that has been claimed to be the major driver for organizational members to engage in spiritual practices or activities.

7. "...a committed volunteer or social entrepreneur is more likely to work hard to create value through his activities than someone who holds a job merely to earn a paycheck" (Frumkin, 2002:23), an assertion completely in line with organizational benefits claims being offered for SAW. It has also been empirically found that the non-profit employees emphasized serving the public needs over extrinsic rewards like a sizeable income (Wittmer, 1991).

8. Another review of literature connected to motivation of non-profit sector employees in general and teaching and hospital staff in particular concluded that the motivation factors for employees in non-profits may be different from those for for-profit organizations (Schepers et al., 2005). The motivational factors –in consonance with SAW literature – were: "a preference for working with and for people, altruism, personal growth, social contacts, opportunities to learn versus more ambition, and intrinsic rewards versus extrinsic rewards like income and money" (Schepers, 2005:203).

A comparison of the nonprofit features with the various features of SAW movement listed above show interesting parallels that strongly suggest the potential utility of the nonprofit sector in examining the assertions advanced by SAW scholars. Consequently, it can be argued that these features would make accessing and researching spiritual issues easier in the non-profit organizations than has been the experience of scholars in mainstream corporate organizations.

After establishing non-profit organizations as fertile grounds for the practice of spirituality in the organizational domain, the essential heterogeneity of the sector (Hansmann, 1987) necessitated marking a theoretical distinction within the non-profit sector to examine the impact of dissimilar contexts in an empirical examination of SAW.

From the perspective of SAW, non-profit organizations can be placed along a continuum of spirituality. On one end would be organizations whose raison-d'être is spirituality. These organizations would consider the religious and spiritual aspirations of their participants as their primary resource and would have come into existence to give expression to the spiritual and religious values of their founders and their supporters. At the other end of the continuum would exist organizations that disown all spiritual issues in their functions and processes and validate their existence based on the service that they provide to their beneficiaries. The latter category of organizations meet the unmet social demands arising out of government and market failures and thus would justify themselves on the basis of their instrumental outcomes.

An empirical examination of SAW along a range of organizations on the explicitly-spiritual to the explicitly-non-spiritual continuum afforded the opportunity to investigate a whole range of issues that SAW scholarship is debating. In particular, the following issues received particular illumination:

1. A central issue in SAW literature has been the place of religion in the study of spirituality at workplace. Scholars have argued both for and against having religion as an organizational feature in supposedly secular settings. The issue of exclusion and discrimination in organizational settings on the basis of one's religious identity has prompted many a SAW scholar to advocate strict boundaries between religion and organizations. A comparison and contrast of member attitudes and work practices in the explicitly-spiritual and explicitly non-spiritual nonprofits provided just the opportunity to examine how the contentious issues of diversity and discrimination are dealt with in the avowedly spiritual and markedly secular organizations.

2. Another issue that has gained considerable attention in SAW literature has been the dichotomy between the instrumental ends towards which SAW is directed versus the assumed non-material nature of SAW outcomes. By focusing attention on these two categories, one of which is marked by the expressive rationale while the other is focused on its instrumental outcomes, a better appreciation of the apparently dichotomous roles of the expressive and instrumental outcomes was made possible.

Further, a section of literature has looked at the importance of fit between organizational values and personal values such that organizations can reap benefits from the practice of spirituality at work (Jurkiewicz & Giacalone, 2004). Thus, it was of interest to examine how the explicit spiritual focus of a few organizations compared with the denial of spiritual issues in others organizations in terms of the conditions available for SAW practice.

3.6 Research Objectives

Drawing from the preceding discussions, it was concluded that the most valuable contribution to literature could be made by having the following as research objectives for this study:

1. To empirically enquire into the antecedents of SAW along three areas: socio-cultural, organizational, and personal;

2. To confirm SAW's conceptualization in three central themes distilled from literature: Integrity/Wholeness, Meaningful work, and Larger than oneself;

3. To study SAW's manifestation in organizations in general and in dissimilar contexts in particular;

4. To explore the suitability of P-O fit lens of organizational behavior for studying SAW;

5. To study the impact of the organizational context for SAW; and

6. To examine the consequences of SAW.

3.7 Research Questions

The research objectives mentioned above led to the following research questions for this study:

6. What are the reasons for organizational employees to take up spirituality at work?

7. How is spirituality at work understood in Indian nonprofit organizations?

8. How is spirituality at work manifested and expressed in Indian nonprofit organizations?

9. Would a better alignment of individual SAW needs and individual perceptions of organizational SAW supplies be related to improved outcomes?

10. Does the organizational context mediate the phenomenon of spirituality at work and, if yes, how is the mediation effected?

It was argued that while some of the above questions could be investigated in a quantitative framework with survey instruments those dealing with the reasons for the phenomenon would need a qualitative framework utilizing interview protocols for an in-depth understanding. The sets of hypotheses to be tested using the survey instruments are presented below.

3.8 Specific Hypotheses

In consonance with extant literature that posits an individual-centered view of SAW and the inter-action-based P-O fit view of SAW that has been argued for in this study, different sets of hypotheses were employed for testing. The first and second sets of hypotheses examined the effect of individual preference for the three central themes of SAW on outcome variables of job satisfaction and three facets of organizational commitment. The third and fourth sets of hypotheses examined the effect of individual perceptions of organizational supplies on the three central themes of SAW on outcome variables of job satisfaction and three facets of organizational commitment. Further, fifth and sixth sets of hypotheses tested the additional explanation if any that was brought about by considering the person-organization SAW fit in relation to the two outcome variables.

3.8.1 Individual-based set of hypotheses

Given the extant arguments in literature that highlight the individual SAW needs and their influence on outcomes, the following hypotheses were tested in this study:

H1a: Individual scores on Integrity/Wholeness component of Spirituality at Work would be positively related to Job satisfaction.

H1b: Individual scores on Meaningful work component of Spirituality at Work would be positively related to Job satisfaction.

H1c: Individual scores on Larger than oneself component of Spirituality at Work would be positively related to Job satisfaction.

H1d: Composite Individual scores on Spirituality at Work would be positively related to Job satisfaction.

H2.1a: Individual scores on Integrity/Wholeness component of Spirituality at Work would be positively related to Organizational affective commitment.

H2.1b: Individual scores on Meaningful work component of Spirituality at Work would be positively related to Organizational affective commitment.

H2.1c: Individual scores on Larger than oneself component of Spirituality at Work would be positively related to Organizational affective commitment.

H2.1d: Composite Individual scores on Spirituality at Work would be positively related to Organizational affective commitment.

H2.2a: Individual scores on Integrity/Wholeness component of Spirituality at Work would be positively related to Organizational continuance commitment.

H2.2b: Individual scores on Meaningful work component of Spirituality at Work would be positively related to Organizational continuance commitment.

H2.2c: Individual scores on Larger than oneself component of Spirituality at Work would be positively related to Organizational continuance commitment.

H2.2d: Composite Individual scores on Spirituality at Work would be positively related to Organizational continuance commitment.

H2.3a: Individual scores on Integrity/Wholeness component of Spirituality at Work would be positively related to Organizational normative commitment.

H2.3b: Individual scores on Meaningful work component of Spirituality at Work would be positively related to Organizational normative commitment.

H2.3c: Individual scores on Larger than oneself component of Spirituality at Work would be positively related to Organizational normative commitment.

H2.3d: Composite Individual scores on Spirituality at Work would be positively related to Organizational normative commitment.

3.8.2 Organization-based set of hypotheses

Given the extant arguments in literature that highlight the organizational SAW supplies and their influence on outcomes, the following hypotheses were tested in this study:

H3a: Organizational scores on Integrity/Wholeness component of Spirituality at Work would be positively related to Job satisfaction.

H3b: Organizational scores on Meaningful work component of Spirituality at Work would be positively related to Job satisfaction.

H3c: Organizational scores on Larger than oneself component of Spirituality at Work would be positively related to Job satisfaction.

H3d: Composite Organizational scores on Spirituality at Work would be positively related to Job satisfaction.

H4.1a: Organizational scores on Integrity/Wholeness component of Spirituality at Work would be positively related to Organizational affective commitment.

H4.1b: Organizational scores on Meaningful work component of Spirituality at Work would be positively related to Organizational affective commitment.

H4.1c: Organizational scores on Larger than oneself component of Spirituality at Work would be positively related to Organizational affective commitment.

H4.1d: Composite Organizational scores on Spirituality at Work would be positively related to Organizational affective commitment.

H4.2a: Organizational scores on Integrity/Wholeness component of Spirituality at Work would be positively related to Organizational continuance commitment.

H4.2b: Organizational scores on Meaningful work component of Spirituality at Work would be positively related to Organizational continuance commitment.

H4.2c: Organizational scores on Larger than oneself component of Spirituality at Work would be positively related to Organizational continuance commitment.

H4.2d: Composite Organizational scores on Spirituality at Work would be positively related to Organizational continuance commitment.

H4.3a: Organizational scores on Integrity/Wholeness component of Spirituality at Work would be positively related to Organizational normative commitment.

H4.3b: Organizational scores on Meaningful work component of Spirituality at Work would be positively related to Organizational normative commitment.

H4.3c: Organizational scores on Larger than oneself component of Spirituality at Work would be positively related to Organizational normative commitment.

H4.3d: Composite Organizational scores on Spirituality at Work would be positively related to Organizational normative commitment.

3.8.3 Person-organization fit based set of hypotheses
Given this study's arguments for utilizing the P-O fit perspective to examine SAW and its consequences, the following hypotheses were tested:

H5a: P-O fit scores on Integrity/Wholeness component of Spirituality at Work would be positively related to Job satisfaction.

H5b: P-O fit scores on Meaningful work component of Spirituality at Work would be positively related to Job satisfaction.

H5c: P-O fit scores on Larger than oneself component of Spirituality at Work would be positively related to Job satisfaction.

H5d: Composite P-O fit scores on Spirituality at Work would be positively related to Job satisfaction.

H6.1a: P-O fit scores on Integrity/Wholeness component of Spirituality at Work would be positively related to Organizational affective commitment.

H6.1b: P-O fit scores on Meaningful work component of Spirituality at Work would be positively related to Organizational affective commitment.

H6.1c: P-O fit scores on Larger than oneself component of Spirituality at Work would be positively related to Organizational affective commitment.

H6.1d: Composite P-O fit scores on Spirituality at Work would be positively related to Organizational affective commitment.

H6.2a: P-O fit scores on Integrity/Wholeness component of Spirituality at Work would be positively related to Organizational continuance commitment.

H6.2b: P-O fit scores on Meaningful work component of Spirituality at Work would be positively related to Organizational continuance commitment.

H6.2c: P-O fit scores on Larger than oneself component of Spirituality at Work would be positively related to Organizational continuance commitment.

H6.2d: Composite P-O fit scores on Spirituality at Work would be positively related to Organizational continuance commitment.

H6.3a: P-O fit scores on Integrity/Wholeness component of Spirituality at Work would be positively related to Organizational normative commitment.

H6.3b: P-O fit scores on Meaningful work component of Spirituality at Work would be positively related to Organizational normative commitment.

H6.3c: P-O fit scores on Larger than oneself component of Spirituality at Work would be positively related to Organizational normative commitment.

H6.3d: Composite P-O fit scores on Spirituality at Work would be positively related to Organizational normative commitment.

3.8.4 Examination of the importance of context on organizational SAW supplies perceptions

The implied assertion in the arguments offered thus far on the extant disavowal of context and the importance of considering it for an examination of SAW was that the context would significantly affect the individual perception of organizational SAW supplies. Further, the distinction that was sought out within the domain of nonprofit organizations was that of organizations for whom spirituality was their raison-d'être and those for whom it was not. It was thought only reasonable to expect that the organizations with spirituality as their mission would provide environments that are more conducive for meeting individuals' spiritual aspirations. To that end, the relevant hypothesis stated:

H7: There is a significant difference in favor of explicitly-spiritual organizations in terms of individual perceptions of organizational SAW supplies.

3.9 Conceptual Framework

Figure 3.1 depicts the fundamental conceptual framework that emerged for this study. It provides the background to examine how individual needs for SAW and individual perception of organizational SAW supplies interact to provide the perception of a match that lead to the consequences of job satisfaction and organizational commitment. The framework provides the overall perspective to first enquire into the antecedent factors that prompt individuals to take up SAW. Thereafter, the influence of individual needs and individual perception of organizational supplies on each of the three dimensions of SAW individually and collectively are related to employee's job satisfaction and organizational commitment. It then posits an individual-level and organization-level study of relating SAW needs and SAW supplies to the consequences of job satisfaction and organizational commitment. The interaction between the two levels is investigated next to see if person-organization fit explains employee job satisfaction and organizational commitment beyond that explained by individual SAW needs and organizational SAW supplies individually.

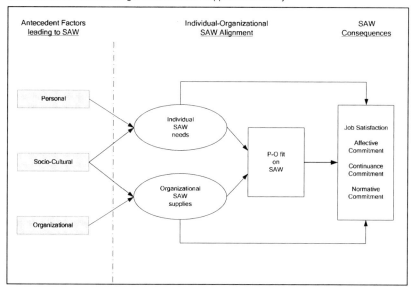

Figure 1: Conceptual framework for the Study

The next chapter shall first summarize the current state of SAW literature on an appropriate methodology to be followed for investigating spirituality at work, drawing directions for this study. It shall be followed up with the actual methodology adopted for this study – including the choice of sample organizations and respondents, measures adopted for the different variables, procedure for collecting data, and the method of data analysis.

Chapter 4: Methodology

The previous chapter outlined the conceptual framework for the present study. The focus of the current chapter will be on the research methodology used for studying SAW. To that end, the following sections shall examine the methodological issues and challenges in studying SAW, an appropriate research design to study SAW, sample selection, measurement of variables, data collection techniques employed, and the data analysis plan.

4.1 Challenges in studying SAW

It is generally agreed that the field of SAW is challenging for researchers, both conceptually and methodologically. These challenges stem from various sources, the most complex of which is the perceived 'un-research-ability' of the topic! It can be argued that an anecdote cited by Eileen Barker (1995:287), though in a slightly different context [at the Annual Meeting for the Scientific Study of Religion at Raleigh, NC, November 1993], may well have taken place in an Academy of Management's Management, Spirituality and Religion meeting:

> The video [shown by Lewis Carter at the 1985 SSSR meeting] started with someone holding a microphone up to Bhagwan Sri Rajneesh and asking him "What do you think about the Society for the Scientific Study of Religion?" There was a long, a very long, pause. Then the guru raised an eyebrow ever so slightly. "In my whole life," he said, "I don't think I've ever heard of anything so ridiculous."

Bhagwan Sri Rajneesh's comment is illustrative of those who argue that the personal and intimate nature of spirituality renders an objective and scientific study impossible. However, various processes and institutions – including religion, from which spirituality is derived - have been researched scientifically. The question that remains to be answered then is not whether spirituality is open to scientific investigation at all, but what could be a more valid way to go about researching into spirituality.

It is in this direction that researchers are made out to face an impediment. While many of the concepts associated with spirituality do not readily lend themselves to the accepted customs of rigorous scholarship, the need to legitimize the field makes such an effort unavoidable. Dean, Fornaciari and McGee (2003) label the debate as a 'relevance versus legitimacy' issue. They argue that even though many of the accepted tools of social science research cannot be applied to the field of SAW without suitable modification, the need for academic legitimacy forces scholars to apply them without much thought. Claiming that the settled organizational research methods based on positivist traditions are inadequate to do justice to the subject matter of SAW, Dean, Fornaciari and McGee (2003: 379) argue:

> It has been generally established that the positivist, empiricist methodological model is not only insufficient for SRW research, but may actually harm the discipline by inauthentically measuring and analyzing crucial SRW variables such as spirit, soul, faith, God, and cosmos...

In addition, the upsurge of interest in SAW leads scholars to confront a curious difficulty of studying and presenting a phenomenon not open to traditional methods of inquiry within established legitimated frameworks (p. 379):

[SAW] research... needs to showcase excellent theoretical, conceptual, and most importantly empirical research, but the legitimated research methods rubric for social science has been shown to lack tools critical to justifiable studies within the SRW research stream.

At root, this is an epistemological issue. Written succinctly, Benefiel (2003, p. 2) wonders whether [SAW] work can be responsibly "measured in units" that are recognized by current scientific paradigms. Arguing that positivist methods are inappropriate and potentially dangerous to [SAW] work is an epistemological claim that how we know, and what we know, in the [SAW] field cannot be plumbed using traditionally accepted empiricist models.

However, the rejection of all academic standards under the excuse of the un-research-ability of the topic also leads many scholars into personal expositions that claim a priori validity. Noting that many of the SAW writers and practitioners are not friendly with the scientific approaches, Gibbons (2000: 125) remarks: "My experience at numerous conferences suggests to me that in their race away from mechanistic and reductionist thinking, they abandon critical thinking as well."

The relevance versus legitimacy debate has also been linked (Benefiel, 2005) to the four paradigms suggested by Burrell and Morgan in their 1994 publication *Sociological Paradigms and Organisational Analysis*. All approaches in organizational studies under the two dimensions of the philosophical standpoint (objective versus subjective) and the theory of society ('sociology of regulation' versus 'sociology of radical change') (Burrell & Morgan, 1979). The dominant functionalist paradigm in organizational research could then be situated within the objective viewpoint while being embedded in the sociology of regulation. Thus, the other three non-dominant paradigms of organizational inquiry were granted a subservient satellite position in organizational studies. As originally proposed, these paradigms cannot be synthesized owing to their location in opposite subjective-objective conceptions of the philosophical approach towards the subject and that about society. The 'paradigm incommensurability' debate could then be related to SAW studies. The studies that have related the practice of SAW to organizational performance and other material outcomes can be placed in the functionalist paradigm against which the ones that call for an "interpretive" treatment of spirituality are found to struggle.

The inadequacy of objective methods to go into SAW issues has been related to spirituality being considered a more private aspect of one's identity (Lips-Wiersma & Mills, 2002). Consequently, Lips-Wiersma argued, discussions involving spirituality would be deemed "more risky" and would therefore require more intimacy than the organizational contexts afford.

What the above analysis hints at is the need for utilizing a more subjective and researcher-subject interaction dependent methodology, which would allow the issues to be discussed in less impersonal manner than is otherwise allowed by the survey-based "objective" research strategies.

Regardless of the anticipated difficulty of researching on SAW, there has been a rise in academic articles on SAW. Benefiel (2003) investigated the assertion that SAW issues cannot be investigated with established methods and identified four distinctive methodological approaches adopted by researchers in examining SAW issues. The following lines outline the four approaches identified by Benefiel, along with her recommendations for each.

1. A *quantitative trail* that is faithful to mainstream management research literature takes the quantitative route to examine the impact of SAW on organizational performance. Studies in this framework (Ashmos & Duchon, 2000 as an example) define spirituality precisely and propose conceptual frames to build measures that would capture its individual, group-level and organizational effects. Regardless of such studies' ability to communicate with the traditional management researchers, they have been criticized for uncritically adopting old methodological models without assessing their fitness for the SAW area (Fornaciari & Dean, 2001).

2. The *broad "why" and "how"* trail (exemplified by Mitroff & Denton, 1999a) combines qualitative and quantitative methods to propose a managerial conceptual frame and a best practice model for organizations. However, Benefiel recommends that this path too needs to be supplemented with narratives of lived spirituality in organizations and provision of details on the spiritual side of the picture would help put the "best practice" model into practice.

3. The third *deep "how" and "why" trail* is marked by qualitative research exploring operational understanding of spirituality's expression in organizations and its impact on individuals and organizations. Further extensive testing in various organizational contexts would enable the researchers to find if the models produced by this trail apply elsewhere.

4. The final *radical "how" and "why" trail* seeks to go beyond mainstream management theories' focus within and on organizations to locate them in a societal framework towards which they owe certain responsibility. It is not surprising to find literature in this trail to assert that the organizational mission ought to be spiritual uplift of all its stakeholders. Further, beyond the instrumental reasons, this literature would also support that argument that SAW ought to be practiced for its own sake and be valued for spiritual transformation's importance by itself.

Another study (Fornaciari & Dean, 2003) examined the empirical approaches used during the foundational years of SAW literature (1996-2000). The authors concluded that irrespective of the concerns that methodological innovations may perhaps be necessary to study SAW, diverse and dynamic methods were already being used in the field. A significant distribution of the empirical studies in these years were quantitative in nature; employed primary data for primarily cross-sectional studies; were skewed towards large sample sizes; and largely offered conclusive findings. Wary of the struggle between relevance and legitimacy in nascent fields, however, led them to warn that the methodological approaches used in the adolescent years of SAW work, say 2001 to 2006, may well indicate that the field would ossify around "timeworn quantitative methods."

It seems, therefore, that any empirical study ought to walk the fine line between relevance and legitimacy. To that end, a number of measures seem justified:

Faced with the ongoing debate about the difficulties with defining spirituality and SAW, leads could be taken from the extant SAW studies in terms of identifying the central features of SAW. Care should however be exercised that the definitions are not offered obsessively (Dean et al., 2003) and that sufficient latitude is available to elicit and incorporate the respondents' sense of the term.

Further, with doubts on the appropriateness of purely quantitative methods in organizational contexts for investigating SAW, these could be supplemented by incorporation of qualitative data collection techniques. However, to prevent the charge of abandonment of critical thinking (Gibbons, 2000a) the researcher ought to uphold the advocated methodological rigor in the approach that is adopted.

4.2 Research Design

The discussion above could be summed up with the observation that while the functionalist paradigm forces a quantitative testing of hypothesized relationships based on current research, the interpretive paradigm suggests a more accommodative approach to respect the unique experiences of SAW research respondents. This study argues therefore that given the current state of academic churning in SAW research, the best contribution that can be made is by making a two-pronged attack on the problem.

An appropriate empirical research design in SAW would then need to include both quantitative and qualitative research methods to benefit from the strengths of each while making up for their drawbacks. The quantitative approach would allow testing of hypothesized relationships among predefined and measurable variables emerging from previous research. The qualitative approach, on the other hand, would help explore the reasons for these relationships and perhaps also throw up certain features that have not yet been included in existing theory (Punch, 1998).

In this context, it is instructive to look at the various research strategy choices available to address various research questions. Yin (1989) recommends that a survey strategy is appropriate for whom, what, where, how many, and how much research questions whereas the case study is specifically suited for addressing the how and why research questions. In both cases, no control is required over behavioral events and the focus remains on contemporary events. Further, case studies are distinguished by their examining contemporary phenomena in their real-life context when the boundaries between phenomenon and its context are not clear (Yin, 1981). Suggested when the researcher is interested in addressing the "how" and "why" dimensions of the phenomenon, the case studies seem particularly well suited for this inquiry. Given the combination of this study's research questions that called for incorporation of both qualitative and quantitative methods, it was felt that a case study methodology would suit the purposes of this study best. The case study methodology in its ability to incorporate various data collection methods - survey-based quantitative data as well as qualitative evidence from interviews and observations - allowed the best possible combination to study the issues under examination. The argument was further strengthened because all the three arguments for the choice of case study strategy (Russ-Eft & Preskill, 2001) were fulfilled by this study:

1. The phenomenon of spirituality at work was to be explored in its natural setting;

2. The particulars, uniqueness, and diversity of each experience needed to be understood; and

3. Manipulation or contrivance of the phenomenon was inappropriate.

In the paragraphs that follow, specific methodological details about the choice of organizations, choice of respondents, and measurement of variables shall be outlined in detail.

4.3 Sample Selection

4.3.1 Choice of organizations

Owing to empirical evidence from literature that mainstream corporate organizations did not provide a conducive environment for discussions on spirituality, the earlier chapters have argued for the choice of non-profit organizations for this study. This position was further validated by the survey that was conducted amongst the Management Development Program participants at IIM Calcutta. The researcher sought to utilize Mitroff and Denton's instrument

Further, following the study's argument that organizations could vary in opportunities available for the practice of SAW, it was decided to distinguish between organizations based on their spiritual focus. Within this differentiation, one category of non-profits was characterized by a clearly spiritual focus whereas the others were non-profits but did not have a clearly spiritual orientation.

A major issue in choosing prospective respondent organizations for this study was the proper identification of explicitly spiritual and explicitly non-spiritual organizations. However, no study in SAW literature recommended specific organizational characteristics that would enable a researcher to place an organization as being spiritual or otherwise. A particular study had earlier considered the same question for religious organizations to infer that literature provides no consensus on characteristics based on which organizations can be judged religious (Jeavons, 1998). Jeavons (1998) had then gone on to propose seven basic aspects of an organization as an indicator of its religious nature to contrast between religious and secular organizations:

1. Organizational self-identity: Does the choice of a name clearly link the organizaiton to a specific religious tradition?

2. Organizational participants and their inclusion: Are the religious beliefs of participants relevant to the primary purpose of the organization, thus becoming the source of (self)-selection?

3. Source of material resources: Does the organization's religious identity control the availability and acquisition of material resources?

4. Religious nature of goals, products, and services: Does the organization incorporate "spiritual technologies" such as prayer and worship in the production process or service delivery?

5. Organizational information processing and decision making: Are the actual organizational processes being affected or shaped by religious ideals and issues?

6. Organizational power: Is the organizational power derived from either religious sources of power or distributed and exercised in accord with religious values and ideals? and

7. Organizational Fields: Does the focal organization primarily associate and interact with other organizations in a religious organizational field?

This study argued that the typology developed by Jeavons (1998) to identify and contrast religious and secular organizations could be fruitfully extended to identify explicitly spiritual and explicitly non-spiritual non-profit organizations.

Further, since the study utilized organizational commitment and job satisfaction as outcome variables it was necessary to invoke a distinction between volunteers and full-time workers in our choice of organizations. To bring together a sizeable sample of full-time respondents from each organization, care was exercised to shortlist only those organizations that had at least 30 full-time members, as against many other non-profits that primarily involved volunteers. Thus, based on the Jeavons' typology and in accordance with the suggestion that examples of polar types be chosen to contrast the two organization types, seven renowned organizations each in the two sectors were approached for site access. They were provided with a broad outline of the research and confidentiality was promised for respondents. Consequently, three organizations each were chosen to compare the explicitly spiritual and explicitly non-spiritual non-profit organizations in this study.

4.3.2 Choice of respondents

After receiving permissions for data access, each organization was asked to provide the name of a contact person who would be able to help prepare a list of prospective respondents, arrange for appointments with the respondents and ensure availability of archival data for analysis purposes. Each contact person was asked to ensure acceptable representation across various age levels, hierarchy, education levels and tenure in the organization in the shortlist of prospective respondents to capture a representative view from the entire organization. In three organizations, it was necessary to call a general meeting and brief the organizational members about the purpose of the study. The attempt was to get around thirty respondents from each organization so that the total sample size reached 180 across six organizations.

4.3.2.1 Final sample of respondents

Since the unit of analysis in the study was the individual, the sample of respondents comprised the individuals who agreed to data collection after being identified by their respective organization's contact persons. The final sample consisted of 179 respondents, from six organizations. After the data was subjected to the usual data-cleaning operations to take care of the issues of outliers in variable values, the study continued with a final sample of 169 respondents. Details of the finally used respondents from various organizations according to their age groups, educational qualifications, and tenure in organizations are given in Tables 4.1, 4.2, and 4.3 respectively.

It has been mentioned in the previous chapter that data was collected by the researcher personally from six non-profit organizations, of which three were explicitly spiritual. In all, 179 respondents participated in the quantitative survey-based data collection process [of which 169 were found usable after data-cleaning] and 114 interviews were conducted, ranging from 20 to 160 minutes each. Demographic details of the respondents whose data was eventually utilized for the study from various organizations as per their age-groups, educational qualifications, and tenure in organizations are given in Tables 4.1, 4.2, and 4.3 respectively.

Age Group (in years)		Organization ID						Total
		1	2	3	4	5	6	
< 25	Count	3	0	3	0	0	0	6
	% within OrgnID	10.30%	0.00%	14.30%	0.00%	0.00%	0.00%	3.60%
	% of Total sample	1.80%	0.00%	1.80%	0.00%	0.00%	0.00%	3.60%
25 to 35	Count	15	10	9	5	6	17	62
	% within OrgnID	51.70%	34.50%	42.90%	20.00%	17.60%	54.80%	36.70%
	% of Total sample	8.90%	5.90%	5.30%	3.00%	3.60%	10.10%	36.70%
35 to 45	Count	5	12	6	8	14	10	55
	% within OrgnID	17.20%	41.40%	28.60%	32.00%	41.20%	32.30%	32.50%
	% of Total sample	3.00%	7.10%	3.60%	4.70%	8.30%	5.90%	32.50%
45 to 55	Count	6	3	2	8	6	3	28
	% within OrgnID	20.70%	10.30%	9.50%	32.00%	17.60%	9.70%	16.60%
	% of Total sample	3.60%	1.80%	1.20%	4.70%	3.60%	1.80%	16.60%
> 55	Count	0	4	1	4	8	1	18
	% within OrgnID	0.00%	13.80%	4.80%	16.00%	23.50%	3.20%	10.70%
	% of Total sample	0.00%	2.40%	0.60%	2.40%	4.70%	0.60%	10.70%
Total	Count	29	29	21	25	34	31	169

Table 4.1 Organization ID * Age Group cross-tabulation

It can be observed that organization 1 is relatively younger while organization 5 has the oldest sample amongst our respondents. However, except for the two age brackets of less than 25 years and more than 55 years, distribution of the other respondents is similar in all the six organizations.

Education Group ID		Organization ID						Total
		1	2	3	4	5	6	
Till XII Std.	Count	2	0	0	8	2	0	12
	% within OrgnID	6.90%	0.00%	0.00%	32.00%	5.90%	0.00%	7.10%
	% of Total sample	1.20%	0.00%	0.00%	4.70%	1.20%	0.00%	7.10%
Graduation	Count	3	6	12	14	11	7	53
	% within OrgnID	10.30%	20.70%	57.10%	56.00%	32.40%	22.60%	31.40%
	% of Total sample	1.80%	3.60%	7.10%	8.30%	6.50%	4.10%	31.40%
Post-Graduation	Count	17	19	8	2	15	7	68
	% within OrgnID	58.60%	65.50%	38.10%	8.00%	44.10%	22.60%	40.20%
	% of Total sample	10.10%	11.20%	4.70%	1.20%	8.90%	4.10%	40.20%
Professional qualification	Count	2	3	0	0	0	5	10
	% within OrgnID	6.90%	10.30%	0.00%	0.00%	0.00%	16.10%	5.90%
	% of Total sample	1.20%	1.80%	0.00%	0.00%	0.00%	3.00%	5.90%
Doctorate	Count	5	1	1	1	6	12	26
	% within OrgnID	17.20%	3.40%	4.80%	4.00%	17.60%	38.70%	15.40%
	% of Total	3.00%	0.60%	0.60%	0.60%	3.60%	7.10%	15.40%

Table 4.2 Organization ID * Educational Qualifications cross-tabulation

In terms of the educational qualifications of respondents, the picture is not as uniform as the age-group distribution presented in Table 4.1. Organization 4, for instance, is dominated by less educated individuals whereas organization 6 has most number of PhDs in our sample. Otherwise, 53 graduates and 68 post-graduates make the most of our sample (71.60%).

Tenure (in years)		Organization ID						Total
		1	2	3	4	5	6	
< 2	Count	10	6	4	1	3	3	27
	% within OrgnID	34.50%	20.70%	19.00%	4.00%	8.80%	9.70%	16.00%
	% of Total sample	5.90%	3.60%	2.40%	0.60%	1.80%	1.80%	16.00%
2 to 5	Count	8	3	5	1	10	3	30
	% within OrgnID	27.60%	10.30%	23.80%	4.00%	29.40%	9.70%	17.80%
	% of Total sample	4.70%	1.80%	3.00%	0.60%	5.90%	1.80%	17.80%
5 to 10	Count	4	3	7	4	8	8	34
	% within OrgnID	13.80%	10.30%	33.30%	16.00%	23.50%	25.80%	20.10%
	% of Total sample	2.40%	1.80%	4.10%	2.40%	4.70%	4.70%	20.10%
10 to 20	Count	2	11	5	9	8	15	50
	% within OrgnID	6.90%	37.90%	23.80%	36.00%	23.50%	48.40%	29.60%
	% of Total sample	1.20%	6.50%	3.00%	5.30%	4.70%	8.90%	29.60%
> 20	Count	5	6	0	10	5	2	28
	% within OrgnID	17.20%	20.70%	0.00%	40.00%	14.70%	6.50%	16.60%
	% of Total sample	3.00%	3.60%	0.00%	5.90%	3.00%	1.20%	16.60%

Table 4.3 Organization ID * Tenure in organization cross-tabulation

As against the earlier two tables, the overall sample is almost equally distributed among the various tenure-groups. However, a closer examination suggests that organization 3 is populated by respondents who have not had a long tenure in the organization while organization 4 is mostly composed of those who have had a long tenure.

The variation in sample distribution would have an interesting implication for our findings, as shall be discussed in subsequent chapters.

4.4 Data Collection Technique

Considering the objectives of the research that entailed collection of both quantitative and qualitative aspects related to SAW, both survey instruments and a structured interview-protocol were devised to collect data. Details about the questionnaire and the structured interview protocol used in this study are presented in the next section.

4.4.1 Survey instrument questionnaire

Self-report measurements remain the most common form of data collection in organizational behavior research. The most important advantage of self-report instruments is the ability to capture that which is of primary importance in deciding human behavior – individual's perception of one's environment. Thus, amongst the various alternatives for data collection self-report survey instruments are especially well suited when the study probes into perceptions. Further, it also offers the advantage of efficiently collecting data from many people in a short period. The chief drawback of the method, however, is that self-report instruments may not always give accurate information. Individual responses may be biased by internal mood states, social influences of co-workers, or stable internal positions (Spector, 1994). However, advantages and disadvantages are associated with each data collection technique and the use of any one ought to be chiefly dictated by the research question.

The study argued for adoption of P-O fit measure in terms of SAW needs and supplies to relate it to the outcomes variables. Correspondingly, since the quantitative part of the study aimed at understanding the perceptions relating to individual's need for spirituality at work and organizational availability of such supplies to relate them to the outcome variables of job satisfaction and organizational commitment, the primary mode of data collection was a survey instrument.

The instrument designed to measure the variables of this study's conceptual framework is presented in the Appendix. Beyond the demographic data to be collected on the first page, the questionnaire consisted of two parts. The first part assessed the independent variables – individual SAW needs and individual perception of organizational SAW supplies – and the second part explored the organizational commitment and job satisfaction of the individual. The independent variables were measured with scales that had to be constructed for this study based on similar scales that existed in SAW literature. These scaled were then adapted to reflect more accurately the themes utilized in this study. To measure the dependent variables - two of the most commonly used variables in organizational behavior research – choice had to be made amongst the various scales available for their measurement. The following subsections shall detail the independent and dependent variables used, development and utilization of scales used for their measurement, the debate surrounding the measurement of P-O fit and the approach adopted to measure P-O fit in this study.

4.4.1.1 Independent Variables

This study makes an argument for utilizing P-O fit measure for SAW research by comparing and contrasting the individual perceptions about one's own SAW needs and the corresponding organizational supplies of SAW to relate it then with the two outcome variables. It thus became necessary to go into the P-O fit literature in organizational behaviour area to settle the issue of operationalization of P-O fit. Literature on P-O fit suggests two methods for operationalizing P-O fit: direct and indirect measurement (Kristof, 1996).

The direct measurement technique asks the person explicitly if a fit is sensed between oneself and the organization on the characteristic under investigation. Under this technique, a good fit is believed to exist as long as the person reports it does, whether the person and the organization have similar characteristics. However, the direct measurement technique has been critiqued on the score that it confounds individual and organizational characteristics rendering estimation of independent effects difficult (Edwards, 1991).

In contrast, indirect measurement tries to assess actual or objective fit. The person responds to separate scales that measure individual and organizational characteristics separately and then the two scales are compared to emerge with an objective measurement of fit. In this particular process of indirect measurement of P-O fit, measuring organizational characteristics proves to be a tricky issue. In particular, organizational characteristics that are perceptual in nature call for aggregation of individual level data. Further, considerable debate exists on whether the individual level responses ought to display a certain amount of homogeneity before they are clubbed together into an organizational level characteristic. There are arguments on both sides of the argument. On one hand are those who contend that the variance between individual scores may be seen as the error term around the true organizational score. Those on the other side of the debate argue that in cases of a perceptual organizational variable, where different subunits may hold varying perceptions of organizational characteristic, one true organizational score may not exist (for a fuller treatment of this debate, refer to Kristof, 1996:12-13).

Then again, there are arguments that for organizational characteristics that are perceptual in nature aggregation of individual level data need not be necessary. Instead, individual level measures of both the individual characteristics and individual *perceptions* of organizational characteristics would suffice, owing to the fact that it is not the objective reality out there that drives one's beliefs and behavior but one's own perceptions of it. Therefore, it is the individual perceptions of the organizational characteristic that would have a stronger influence on satisfaction, commitment and the like.

Consequently, this study sided with the approach of utilizing individual perception of organizational SAW supplies to measure fit. This decision was taken based on the findings that such an approach holds, in particular, for assessing the fit on difficult-to-measure characteristics like values or goals as is the case with the 'spirituality at work' construct (Kristof, 1996).

In the two sections that follow a brief detail shall be provided about scale construction for the two independent variables.

4.4.1.1.1 Individual needs for SAW

As discussed earlier in section 2.3.2, this variable tries to capture the individual's needs on the three SAW themes that have been distilled from literature: integrity and wholeness; meaningful work; and larger than oneself. Each one of these three themes was then operationally defined. Extensive review of literature on these three themes led to a bank of 36 items indicating individual SAW needs. These items were examined for face and content validity by two professors from the Thesis Advisory Committee, two doctoral students, and two senior functionaries of the target respondent organizations. Based on intensive discussions, this list was finally pruned to nine items for each theme leading to 27 items. A sample item for the integrity and wholeness theme reads as follows: "My organization should enable me to integrate my spiritual life with my work life." Thus, on each one of 27 statements the respondents chose an option on a 5-point Likert scale ranging from 1=Strongly disagree to 5=Strongly agree. Average scores on the nine statements for each theme separately gave the individual preference for that particular theme of SAW and the overall average provided the overall individual SAW need score. Care was taken to reverse code and randomize the statements in the final instrument.

4.4.1.1.2 Organizational supplies of SAW

Owing to the potential use of individual SAW needs and organizational SAW supplies variables for calculating P-O SAW fit it was necessary to consult P-O fit literature on the suggestions for scale construction. The overwhelming suggestion for ensuring mutual relevance of characteristics under investigation makes it imperative that the measurement be commensurate, implying thereby that both person and organization be described with the same content dimensions (Kristof, 1996). Kristof (1996: 10) gives an example of commensurate questions: "How much pay do you receive?" and "How much pay would you like to receive?"

Consequently, each one of the 27 statements for individual SAW needs measurement was changed suitably to reflect organizational SAW supplies. For instance, the matching item for the integrity and wholeness theme statement referred in the earlier subsection read, "My organization enables me to integrate my spiritual life with my work life."

4.4.1.2 Dependent variables

The consequences of SAW have remained the source of considerable debate in literature as mentioned in previous chapters. This study sought to examine the impact of P-O fit on SAW on two outcome variables as discussed below.

4.4.1.2.1 Organizational Commitment

Section 3.4.2 has earlier looked at the reason for the popularity of organizational commitment in industrial and organizational psychology. Organizational commitment essentially is the extent to which individuals feel attached or committed towards their employing organization and the degree to which they would like to preserve membership. The concept of organizational commitment was refined by Meyer and Allen (1997)who argued there could be three different parts of organizational commitment: affective, continuance, and normative. Affective commitment suggests the extent to which the employee emotionally identifies with the organization and *wants* to continue with it. Continuance commitment results from awareness about the costs of leaving the organization and thus points to the *need* to continue. Normative commitment owes itself to a feeling of obligation to continue with the organization and is associated with a feeling that the employee *ought* to remain with the organization.

As is the case with job satisfaction, several scales are available for measuring organizational commitment. The first such measure to be developed Organizational Commitment Questionnaire (Mowday, Steers, & Porter, 1979) faces the primary criticism that it focuses only on the affective part of organizational commitment with less information being available on continuance and normative commitment. In contrast, considerable evidence is available on the desirable psychometric properties of Meyer and Allen's three-component model of organizational commitment (Meyer & Allen, 1997) about its internal and construct validity. [A sample item on normative commitment reads: "This organization deserves my loyalty."] The responses are recorded on a five-point Likert-scale.

4.4.1.2.2 Job Satisfaction

As discussed earlier in section 3.4.1, job satisfaction is the most commonly used attitudinal variable in industrial and organizational psychology. Not surprisingly, many scales with proven reliability and validity are readily available to assess job satisfaction. The uni-dimensional Faces Scale (Kunin, 1955) where individuals indicate how they feel about their job in general by choosing one among the six faces; the Job Descriptive Index developed by Patricia Cain Smith and her colleagues (Smith, 1975); Minnesota Satisfaction Questionnaire from a team of researchers in the University of Minnesota (Weiss, Dawis, England, & Lofquist, 1967); and Spector's Job Satisfaction Survey (JSS) (Spector, 1997).

For this study, we chose to use the Spector's Job Satisfaction Survey as its validity and reliability has been established in prior researches. Further, the scale can be freely adapted and modified for any research study.

As is typical of all job satisfaction measures, JSS consists of various items that represent statements about the person's job or job situation representing nine facets of the job: pay, promotion, supervision, fringe benefits, contingent rewards, operating conditions, co-workers, nature of work, and communication. [A sample item of the JSS about co-workers reads: "I find I have to work harder at my job because of the incompetence of people I work with."] Scores on the various statements can then be added together to result in a single Job Satisfaction score. While a six-point Likert scale was used in the original JSS for 36 items, the scale was revised to 18 items – 2 items per job facet – for the sake of parsimony. Responses were recorded on a 5-point Likert scale ranging from 1=Strongly disagree to 5=Strongly agree to maintain consistency with the other scales of the questionnaire.

4.4.2 Interview protocol

It has been mentioned earlier that this study used both a survey-based data collection instrument to collect quantitative data and an interview protocol to access the subjective reality as sensed by organizational members. Based on an extensive review of SAW literature, it was decided to focus on four aspects to address the relevant research questions of this study: 1. Organizational choices and incidents; 2. Organizational issues; 3. Spirituality; and 4. Spirituality at work. The structured interview protocol used for the study is provided in the Appendix.

Nine questions in the first section of organizational choices and incidents concerned itself with the personal and organizational antecedents of SAW. In particular, it went into the reasons for individual choice for joining the particular organization; other choices available then; early impressions about organizational culture; early socialization processes in the organization; and opinions on the individual's values' fit with the organization. Owing to a frequent argument in literature that SAW is intimately related to one's values (Jurkiewicz & Giacalone, 2004), this section also explored the basic values that guided the respondent's life and if values were being compromised in the workplace.

The second section of organizational issues comprised seven questions and explored the respondent's perceptions of antecedents of organizational commitment by probing into the reasons for the individual's staying back in the organization, what one liked best about it, and if any factors would convince the respondent to leave the organization. The next section engaged with the respondent's opinions of spirituality (4 questions) and its importance to the respondent. This section also explored the dynamic nature of the understanding of spirituality and its change with one's stay in the organization. The last section was the most detailed with 15 questions and it concentrated on the focus of this study: spirituality at work. It elicited responses on issues relating to the perceived relevance of spirituality in the workplace, if it was an appropriate topic for discussion there, and more significantly the respondent's view on how it could be practiced at work. Specific questions sought to list individual and organizational features that would enable the practice of spirituality at work. This part of the interview also explored the incidents that were reflective of SAW's practice at the respondent's organization and the observable or potential consequences emanating from the practice of spirituality in the workplace.

Findings from the data collected through the interview protocol and their implications shall be discussed in following chapters.

4.5 Procedure for data collection and data preparation

Details have been provided earlier in section 4.3.1 about how the respondents were selected for this study. Once a short-list of prospective respondents was prepared appointments were sought with them. The researcher approached them with the questionnaire and the interview protocol. Face to face interviews were conducted with the aid of the structured interview protocol that has been detailed in an earlier section. The interviews' duration ranged from 20 minutes to 160 minutes. In the same meeting, detailed instructions were provided for filling up the questionnaire and clarifications provided. These questionnaires were later collected during subsequent trips to that organization. In many cases when the respondent did not have enough time, it was necessary to have the respondent answer only the questionnaire. Later, all these interviews were converted from cassette-tapes to a digital format and the interviews transcribed. The transcripts were then coded according to the available guidelines (Miles & Huberman, 1994) and categories created according to both literature and data. Details about the points that emerged from interviews shall be summarized in later chapters.

4.6 Data Analysis Plan

As noted earlier, this study utilized both qualitative and quantitative methods for data collection. The quantitative part of data collection entailed administration of a survey instrument that contained 87 questions probing into the individual needs and organizational supplies on the various SAW themes and outcomes of organizational commitment and job satisfaction. The qualitative part of data collection involved administration of a structured interview protocol with 36 questions that explored the respondents' views about the organization's culture, specific organizational incidents, conceptions of spirituality and opinions about SAW.

4.6.1 Quantitative Data analysis

SPSS 13.0 data analysis package was used for descriptive, correlational, MANOVA, ANOVA and multiple regressions analysis procedures. Data analysis was guided by the research questions and the hypotheses to be tested. In particular, the procedures used for answering the various questions were as follows.

The first step in quantitative data analysis involved estimating the internal consistency or reliability of the various scales that had been constructed for the study. This was done at both subscale and scale level. Cronbach's Alpha is the most commonly used internal consistency reliability coefficient. It models internal consistency based on average correlation among scale items. Conventionally, a score of 0.60 is considered acceptable for an exploratory study though a cut-off of 0.70 is asked for by many researchers for a "good" scale.

The calculated Cronbach's alpha reliability coefficients for Individual needs for integrity and wholeness (I_iw), Individual needs for meaningful work (I_mw), Individual needs for larger than oneself (I_lto), Overall Individual needs for SAW (I_SAW), Perceived Organizational supplies of integrity and wholeness (O_iw), Perceived Organizational supplies of meaningful work (O_mw), Perceived Organizational supplies of larger than oneself (O_lto), and

Perceived Overall Organizational supplies of SAW (O_SAW) are provided in Table no. 4.4 below:

Variable	I_iw	I_mw	I_lto	I_SAW	O_iw	O_mw	O_lto	O_SAW
Cronbach's alpha	0.693	0.759	0.770	0.874	0.753	0.781	0.823	0.908

Table 4.4 Cronbach's-alpha reliability coefficients for study's independent variables

Having settled the internal consistency of the scales used, the focus shifted to testing the overall effect of the independent variables on all the outcome variables taken together. Consequently, MANOVA was used to test this effect and that being found significant the hypotheses proposed in the study were tested.

Hypotheses 1 through 6 looked at the relationships of the individual needs and organizational supplies on the various SAW themes, and P-O fit on SAW with the outcome variables of affective organizational commitment, continuance organizational commitment, normative organizational commitment and job satisfaction. The direction and strength of these relationships was tested with Pearson's Product Moment correlation procedure. The significance level was set at .05 and a correlation matrix was calculated to study the relationships between various scores.

Hypotheses that looked at the differences between the two types of organizations – explicitly spiritual and explicitly non-spiritual – were tested by using ANOVA separately for the four outcome variables: affective organizational commitment, continuance organizational commitment, normative organizational commitment and job satisfaction.

Further, hierarchical multiple regression analysis was carried out to isolate the effects of various control variables (Age, tenure in the organization, educational qualification, sex) and analyze the main effects and interaction effects of the various independent variables on one outcome variable at a time. Thus, in all four regression equations were drawn up.

4.6.2 Qualitative Data analysis

As discussed in section 4.4.2, this study also involved administration of a structured interview protocol. Each interview was later transcribed and then coded according the suggestions available for theory elaboration (Vaughan, 1992). Theory elaboration uses previously identified theoretical constructs in an inductive manner to clarify, describe, and more fully specify their relevance for different organizational contexts.

An analytical framework is evolved from literature with "building blocks (categories) and significant sensitizing concepts (properties)" (Vaughan, 1992: 191). Each interview is then analyzed independently in light of the theoretical constructs shortlisted above to add to the richness of later analysis. Eventually, evidence from all the cases together contributes to a final understanding that has gained from both existing theory and empirical data collected. The details of this analysis and its contribution to an understanding of SAW shall be detailed in following chapters.

The next chapter shall elaborate on an analysis of the data collected, and the results obtained for this study.

Chapter 5: Results

The last four chapters have established the rationale for this study, identified the gaps that remain to be filled in the study of SAW, proposed the conceptual framework leading to the specific issues to be examined in this study, and then presented a workable research methodology. This chapter will present the findings from the primary data that was collected from six organizations.

The results are presented in four sections. Section 5.1 presents the overall distribution of data relating to the quantitative section of this research for comparing data across individual organizations and across the two organization types that have been researched in this study. Section 5.2 presents results from quantitative data analysis for hypothesis testing. The third section discusses the findings from in-depth interviews with respondents. The final section summarizes the results obtained.

5.1 Overall distribution of quantitative data

Before getting into the findings from data relating to the various research questions and techniques used to analyze data, a brief summary of the individual scores obtained on study variables is offered below. Table 5.1 presents the means and standard deviations of individual scores on each variable explored in the present study. The data has been put together to compare the scores across the six organizations individually and across the two organizational categories of explicitly-spiritual and other non-profits before presenting the overall scores.

On the whole, it can be observed that Organization Type 2 (explicitly-spiritual organizations with OrgnIDs 4 through 6) consistently score higher than the other organizations not only on the parameters of individual and organizational spirituality but also on the outcome variables. The scores on organizational continuance commitment that are distributed almost the same way across organizations are the sole exception to this observation. The significance or otherwise of these differences shall be explored with a t-test and ANOVA later in the chapter.

Numerical values for Individual preferences for SAW (I_SAW) as measured by this instrument can range from 0 to 5. As can be seen from Table 5.1 respondents from all organizations except for organization no. 5 report a value greater than 4. Further, the scores on all of the three I_SAW sub-scales – integrity and wholeness (I_iw), meaningful work (I_mw), and larger than oneself (I_lto) - too are skewed in the direction of higher preferences. At the sub-scale level, the scores fall below 4 only for the explicitly non-spiritual organizations on the individual needs for integrity and wholeness sub-scale. Overall, the data from the sample indicates high preferences for SAW.

In a similar manner, the scores on availability of organizational supplies (O_SAW) too can range from 0 to 5. While the average for the entire sample was 3.9073 indicating a moderately high availability of organizational supplies, the differences across the two categories of organizations were in favor of explicitly-spiritual organizations. On the various sub-scales for O_SAW too, the scores are in the moderately high region with the lowest sub-scale mean score being 3.3478 and the highest 4.4437.

As far as the outcome variables are concerned, the evidence on organizational continuance commitment is mixed with the overall average from the entire sample being the lowest, at 3.3318. Amongst the outcome variables, the highest overall score is on affective commitment - 4.1207 – which should not be surprising as the spirituality issue under examination is considered largely affective. However, all the outcome variables – affective organizational commitment, continuance organizational commitment, normative organizational commitment, and job satisfaction – range from 3.2870 to 4.5283 and can be considered moderately high to high.

		I_iw	I_mw	I_lto	I_SAW	O_iw	O_mw	O_lto	O_SAW	OC_A	OC_C	OC_N	JS
						Organization-wise distribution of data							
1	Mean (N=29)	3.9534	4.3028	4.5179	4.2576	3.3024	3.7431	3.6586	3.569	3.5931	3.3793	3.7034	3.3738
	Std. Deviation	0.48201	0.38806	0.34092	0.34015	0.5006	0.51709	0.56577	0.46895	0.77179	0.60082	0.62019	0.62321
2	Mean (N=29)	3.9363	4.1993	4.479	4.2055	3.2917	3.7352	3.8121	3.6134	3.8276	3.4897	3.7517	3.4479
	Std. Deviation	0.45208	0.3752	0.37525	0.34127	0.4362	0.37695	0.63832	0.40357	0.66057	0.4916	0.6451	0.44586
3	Mean (N=21)	3.979	4.3343	4.4448	4.2529	3.7576	4.0748	4.3181	4.0481	4.0476	3.2952	4.019	3.8305
	Std. Deviation	0.51167	0.4331	0.42021	0.40257	0.45553	0.58883	0.40096	0.42725	0.6983	0.29407	0.60301	0.41403
4	Mean (N=25)	4.5248	4.7876	4.8632	4.7248	4.348	4.5596	4.7428	4.5492	4.792	3.608	4.584	4.2024
	Std. Deviation	0.51275	0.34593	0.22675	0.272	0.41605	0.39138	0.2958	0.28449	0.46	0.58161	0.52574	0.48203
5	Mean (N=34)	4.117?	4.4806	4.4482	4.3488	3.8529	4.075	4.0035	3.9774	4.3353	3.2118	3.9706	3.6585
	Std. Deviation	0.32377	0.36796	0.39151	0.2863	0.42376	0.43801	0.29557	0.32013	0.38367	0.5186	0.68248	0.44431
6	Mean (N=31)	4.2661	4.3406	4.3335	4.3126	4.0103	4.0648	4.1081	4.0603	4.5161	3.2258	4.2452	3.7294
	Std. Deviation	0.46438	0.54039	0.44227	0.44048	0.56994	0.55731	0.52364	0.50831	0.42198	0.6148	0.54335	0.528
						Organization Type-wise distribution of data							
1	Mean (N=79)	3.9547	4.2732	4.4842	4.2372	3.4195	3.8284	3.8903	3.7127	3.8	3.3975	3.8051	3.5224
	Std. Deviation	0.47345	0.39503	0.37202	0.35425	0.5034	0.5081	0.61147	0.47523	0.72678	0.49458	0.63081	0.53904
2	Mean (N=90)	4.2817	4.5177	4.524	4.4408	4.0447	4.2061	4.2449	4.1648	4.5244	3.3267	4.2356	3.834
	Std. Deviation	0.45771	0.46132	0.42869	0.38388	0.51289	0.51552	0.49682	0.45348	0.45328	0.5909	0.63852	0.53247
						Overall Data Summary							
	Mean (N=169)	4.1288	4.4034	4.5054	4.3456	3.7524	4.0295	4.0791	3.9534	4.1858	3.3598	4.0343	3.6883
	Std. Deviation	0.49176	0.4474	0.40251	0.38302	0.59573	0.54442	0.57952	0.51477	0.69679	0.54754	0.66869	0.55625

Table 5.1 Summary of mean and standard deviation values for each variable

Inter-category organizational differences show a largely consistent trend: the explicitly-spiritual organizations show higher scores not only for all the outcome variables (except for continuance organizational commitment) but also the independent variables of individual needs and organizational supplies of SAW and all their components. Detailed analysis of these differences shall be attempted in section 5.2 with ANOVA.

5.2 Quantitative Data Analysis

Exploratory data analysis was carried out first to examine data at the variable level to test for its adherence to the various assumptions for subsequent quantitative analysis. The data from survey instruments was then utilized to answer the various hypotheses that have been presented earlier in the conceptual framework chapter.

5.2.1 Exploratory data analysis

Before computing any inferential statistics that would test inter-variable hypotheses, it is recommended that the data is checked for its adherence to the various assumptions for statistical analysis (Schwab, 2005). The analysis involves computing multiple descriptive statistics and graphs to verify issues relating to outliers, non-normal distributions and adherence to the assumptions of equality of variance and normality of distribution.

For testing the assumptions of normality for the sample, the categories with ordinal variables were subjected to a descriptive statistics measurement. Results presented in Table 5.2 suggested that none of Respondents' age group (AgeGrpID), Respondents' educational qualifications (EduGpID), and Tenure in organizations (yrsOrgnID) violated the normality assumption. [The skewness was between 1 and -1 for all three variables.] Consequently, the sample distribution can be accepted as being normal for the various demographic variables on which data had been collected.

	N	Minimum	Maximum	Mean	Std.	Skewness	
	Statistic	Statistic	Statistic	Statistic	Statistic	Statistic	Std. Error
AgeGrpID	169	1	5	2.94	1.051	0.493	0.187
EduGpID	169	1	5	2.91	1.128	0.529	0.187
yrsOrgnID	169	1	5	3.13	1.330	-0.226	0.187

Table 5.2 Descriptive statistics for ordinal variables

Further, Boxplots and stem-and-leaf plots were used to examine the outcome variables: job satisfaction (JS), organizational affective commitment (OC_A), organizational continuance commitment (OC_C), and organizational normative commitment (OC_N). [Boxplots are useful for identifying respondents with extreme scores, which can skew the distribution and thus make it non-normal.] Correspondingly, data from ten respondents who contributed outliers on several variables that were utilized for the study were cleaned and the study continued with data from 169 respondents.

For the set of these 169 respondents, there was only one outlier each on OC_A and OC_N, the whiskers were approximately the same length, and the line in the box lay approximately in the middle of the box signifying that the variables were approximately normally distributed. Descriptive statistics of the dependent variables too indicated adherence to the assumptions of various tests as per Table 5.3.

	N	Range	Minimum	Maximum	Mean	Std.	Skewness	
	Statistic	Statistic	Statistic	Statistic	Statistic	Statistic	Statistic	Std. Error
OC_A	169	2.80	2.20	5.00	4.1858	.69679	-.795	.187
OC_C	169	2.80	2.00	4.80	3.3598	.54754	-.100	.187
OC_N	169	3.00	2.00	5.00	4.0343	.66869	-.438	.187
JS	169	2.50	2.33	4.83	3.6883	.55625	-.058	.187

Table 5.3 Descriptive statistics for dependent variables

It can be observed that the skewness values for all the four dependent variables are between -1 and +1, indicating that the distributions are approximately normal.

Moreover, given that the statistical tests that were to be applied in this study assumed a linear relationship between variables, it was necessary to test the data for linearity. The matrix scatterplot provided a pictorial depiction of the relationship between the variables and the clusters were examined for the assumption of linearity. In this test, if a straight line can be drawn so that most of the data points lie relatively close to it, we can assume that the two variables are related in a linear fashion. However, if the cluster appears to be creating a curve, rather than a straight line, it would imply a non-linear relationship between the two variables to analyze which non-linear analyses would be required. It was found that the variables exhibited a linear relationship and thus a suitable transformation, to meet the linearity assumptions, was not required.

The same scatterplot also tested for assumptions of homoscedasticity and it was found that the assumption was not violated by the variables utilized in this study.

5.2.2 Multivariate Statistical tests

Before going into the individual associational analyses on specific variables it is recommended that all the outcome variables be examined simultaneously for effect of the various independent variables. MANOVA is utilized when two or more normal (scale) statistically and conceptually related dependent variables are analyzed simultaneously. Only if the effect is significant on all outcome variables considered together is the data examined for significant relationships at the level of individual variables. Individual ANOVAs are to be computed only if the multivariate (MANOVA) results are significant.

The assumptions for MANOVA that were sustained by present data include: independent observations, multivariate normality, and homogeneity of variance, although MANOVA as a procedure is robust to violations of normality and homogeneity of variance, provided the groups are of almost equal size (the largest N is no more than 1.5 times the N of the smallest group) (Leech, 2005).

Prior to conducting the multivariate analysis of variance, the respondents were divided into four groups based on their individual SAW needs and organizational SAW supplies scores. Their individual SAW needs scores were divided into two: those above the mean score and those below the mean score of I_{saw} [I_h and I_l respectively]. Similarly, the respondents were also classified into O_{high} and O_{low} scores based on their O_{saw} score being above or below the O_{saw} mean score. Thereafter, a multivariate analysis of variance was conducted to assess if there were differences between the four groups [$I_{high}*O_{high}$; $I_{high}*O_{low}$; $I_{low}*O_{high}$; and $I_{low}*O_{low}$], and whether there was an interaction between the individual SAW needs scores and organizational SAW supplies score, on a linear combination of Job satisfaction, organizational affective commitment, organizational continuance commitment, and organizational normative commitment scores.

Effect	Value		F	Hypothesis df	Error df	Sig.	Partial Eta Squared
Intercept	Wilks' Lambda	.009	4300.601(a)	4.000	162.000	.000	.991
I_hl	Wilks' Lambda	.936	2.755(a)	4.000	162.000	.030	.064
O_hl	Wilks' Lambda	.664	20.505(a)	4.000	162.000	.000	.336
I_hl*O_hl	Wilks' Lambda	.972	1.176(a)	4.000	162.000	.323	.028

a Exact statistic
Design: Intercept+I_hl+O_hl+I_hl * O_hl
Table 5.4 Multivariate test

It can be seen from Table 5.4 that the interaction effect was not significant [Wilks' Lambda = .972, F(4, 162) = 1.176, p = .323, multivariate eta squared = .028]. The main effect for individual SAW needs was significant [Wilks' Lambda = .936, F(4, 162) = 2.755, p = .030, multivariate eta squared = .064] as was that for organizational SAW supplies [Wilks' Lambda = .664, F(4, 162) = 20.505, p = .000, multivariate eta squared = .336]. This indicates that not only does the linear composite differ for individual SAW needs, it also differs for organizational SAW supplies.

[It may be important to note that the major MANOVA assumption of homogeneity of variances was not violated for any of the dependent variables in the Levene's test.]

Source	Dependent Variable	df	Mean Square	F	Eta value	Sig.
I_hl	OC_A	1	3.140	8.822	0.2258	.003
	OC_C	1	.005	.018	0.0000	.895
	OC_N	1	2.122	6.244	0.1897	.013
	JS	1	.520	2.843	0.1304	.094
O_hl	OC_A	1	9.885	27.772	0.3795	.000
	OC_C	1	.039	.127	0.0316	.722
	OC_N	1	8.845	26.034	0.3688	.000
	JS	1	13.642	74.554	0.5577	.000
I_hl * O_hl	OC_A	1	.008	.022	0.0000	.883
	OC_C	1	.002	.008	0.0000	.929
	OC_N	1	.092	.270	0.0447	.604
	JS	1	.669	3.655	0.1483	.058
Error	OC_A	165	.356			
	OC_C	165	.305			
	OC_N	165	.340			
	JS	165	.183			

Table 5.5 Follow-up ANOVA for the multivariate test

Follow-up ANOVA tests indicate that effects of individual SAW needs was significant for affective organizational commitment [F(3, 165)=8.822, p=.003] and normative organizational commitment [F(3, 165)=6.244, p=.013]. Similarly, the effect of organizational SAW supplies was also significant for both affective organizational commitment [F(3, 165)=27.772, p=.000] and normative organizational commitment [F(3, 165)=26.034, p=.000]. However, neither of the two effects was significant for continuance organizational commitment. For Job Satisfaction, the individual SAW needs score was not significant [F(3, 165)=2.843, p=.094] while that on organizational SAW supplies was [F(3, 165)=74.554, p=.000]. The interaction effect of individual SAW needs and Organizational SAW supplies was close to statistical significance for only Job Satisfaction [F(3, 165)=3.655, p=.058] and insignificant for the other three outcome variables relating to organizational commitment. Implications of this intriguing finding shall be explored further in the next chapter.

Once the overall effect of the two main variables and their interaction had been established for a combination of the outcome variables, several subsequent analyses were conducted for each individual outcome variable.

5.2.3 Correlation-based test of hypotheses

First, to explore the strength and direction of relationships between the various variables, correlations were computed for the various variables utilized in this study. Tables 5.6 through 5.8 show the correlation matrix for sub-scale and scale-level independent variables, the sub-scale and scale-level difference scores, and the four outcome variables. In terms of the research hypotheses, the results are as under:

5.2.3.1 Individual-based set of hypotheses

The relationship between Individual needs for SAW and the four outcome variables is presented in Table 5.6 through a correlation matrix. The corresponding hypotheses along with their results follow (Results indicated in parentheses):

	Mean	Std. Dev.	OC_A	OC_C	OC_N	JS
I_iw	4.1288	0.49176	.444(**)	0.07	.417(**)	.425(**)
I_mw	4.4034	0.4474	.438(**)	0.08	.454(**)	.464(**)
I_lto	4.5054	0.40251	.311(**)	.187(*)	.352(**)	.355(**)
I_SAW	4.3456	0.38302	.470(**)	0.127	.479(**)	.487(**)
OC_A	4.1858	0.69679	1	-0.002	.532(**)	.595(**)
OC_C	3.3598	0.54754		1	.192(*)	-0.013
OC_N	4.0343	0.66869			1	.508(**)
JS	3.6883	0.55625				1

** Correlation is significant at the 0.01 level (2-tailed).
* Correlation is significant at the 0.05 level (2-tailed).

Table 5.6 Correlation matrix for individual-based hypotheses

H1a: Individual scores on integrity and wholeness component of Spirituality at Work would be positively related to Job satisfaction. [Supported. Significant positive relationship as per Pearson r correlation coefficient (r=0.425, p<.01, N=169) The positive coefficient indicates that the individuals having a high score on integrity and wholeness component of SAW needs would tend to have a high job satisfaction score and vice versa. The r squared indicates that approximately 18% of the variance in job satisfaction scores can be predicted from the individual's score on integrity and wholeness SAW needs.]

H1b: Individual scores on Meaningful work component of Spirituality at Work would be positively related to Job satisfaction. [Supported. Significant positive relationship as per Pearson r correlation coefficient (r=0.464, p<.01, N=169) The positive coefficient indicates that the individuals having a high score on meaningful work component of SAW needs would tend to have a high job satisfaction score and vice versa. The r squared indicates that approximately 21.5% of the variance in job satisfaction scores can be predicted from the individual's score on meaningful work SAW needs.]

H1c: Individual scores on Larger than oneself component of Spirituality at Work would be positively related to Job satisfaction. [Supported. Significant positive relationship as per Pearson r correlation coefficient (r=0.355, p<.01, N=169) The positive coefficient indicates that the individuals having a high score on larger than oneself component of SAW needs would tend to have a high job satisfaction score and vice versa. The r squared indicates that approximately 12.6% of the variance in job satisfaction scores can be predicted from the individual's score on larger than oneself SAW needs.]

H1d: Composite Individual scores on Spirituality at Work would be positively related to Job satisfaction. [Supported. Significant positive relationship as per Pearson r correlation coefficient (r=0.487, p<.01, N=169) The positive coefficient indicates that the individuals having a high score on individual SAW needs would tend to have a high job satisfaction score and vice versa. The r squared indicates that approximately 23.7% of the variance in job satisfaction scores can be predicted from the individual's composite score SAW needs.]

H2.1a: Individual scores on Integrity/Wholeness component of Spirituality at Work would be positively related to Organizational affective commitment. [Supported. Significant positive relationship as per Pearson r correlation coefficient (r=0.444, p<.01, N=169) The positive coefficient indicates that the individuals having a high individual score on integrity and wholeness SAW need would tend to have a high Organizational affective commitment score and vice versa. The r squared indicates that approximately 19.71% of the variance in Organizational affective commitment scores can be predicted from the individual's score on integrity and wholeness component of SAW needs.]

H2.1b: Individual scores on Meaningful work component of Spirituality at Work would be positively related to Organizational affective commitment. [Supported. Significant positive relationship as per Pearson r correlation coefficient (r=0.438, p<.01, N=169) The positive coefficient indicates that the individuals having a high individual score on meaningful work SAW needs would tend to have a high Organizational affective commitment score and vice versa. The r squared indicates that approximately 19.2% of the variance in Organizational affective commitment scores can be predicted from the individual's score on meaningful work component of SAW needs.]

H2.1c: Individual scores on Larger than oneself component of Spirituality at Work would be positively related to Organizational affective commitment. [Supported. Significant positive relationship as per Pearson r correlation coefficient (r=0.311, p<.01, N=169) The positive coefficient indicates that the individuals having a high individual score on larger than oneself SAW needs would tend to have a high Organizational affective commitment score and vice versa. The r squared indicates that approximately 9.67% of the variance in Organizational affective commitment scores can be predicted from the individual's score on larger than oneself component of SAW needs.]

H2.1d: Composite Individual scores on Spirituality at Work would be positively related to Organizational affective commitment. [Supported. Significant positive relationship as per Pearson r correlation coefficient (r=0.470, p<.01, N=169) The positive coefficient indicates that the individuals having a high individual SAW needs score would tend to have a high Organizational affective commitment score and vice versa. The r squared indicates that approximately 22.1% of the variance in Organizational affective commitment scores can be predicted from the individual's composite score on SAW needs.]

H2.2a: Individual scores on Integrity and Wholeness component of Spirituality at Work would be positively related to Organizational continuance commitment. [Not supported.

Insignificant positive relationship as per Pearson r correlation coefficient (r=0.070, p<.366, N=169) The positive coefficient indicates that the individuals having a high individual score on integrity and wholeness SAW needs would tend to have a high Organizational continuance commitment score and vice versa. The r squared indicates that less than 0.5% of the variance in Organizational continuance commitment scores can be predicted from the individual's score on integrity and wholeness component of SAW needs.]

H2.2b: Individual scores on Meaningful work component of Spirituality at Work would be positively related to Organizational continuance commitment. [Not supported. Insignificant positive relationship as per Pearson r correlation coefficient (r=0.080, p<.303, N=169) The positive coefficient indicates that the individuals having a high individual score on meaningful work SAW needs would tend to have a high Organizational continuance commitment score and vice versa. The r squared indicates that slightly higher than 0.6% of the variance in Organizational continuance commitment scores can be predicted from the individual's score on meaningful work component of SAW needs.]

H2.2c: Individual scores on Larger than oneself component of Spirituality at Work would be positively related to Organizational continuance commitment. [Supported. Significant positive relationship as per Pearson r correlation coefficient (r=0.187, p<.015, N=169) The positive coefficient indicates that the individuals having a high individual score on larger than oneself SAW needs would tend to have a high Organizational continuance commitment score and vice versa. The r squared indicates that 3.5% of the variance in Organizational continuance commitment scores can be predicted from the individual's score on larger than oneself component of SAW needs.]

H2.2d: Composite Individual scores on Spirituality at Work would be positively related to Organizational continuance commitment. [Not supported. Insignificant positive relationship as per Pearson r correlation coefficient (r=0.127, p<.1015, N=169) The positive coefficient indicates that the individuals having a high individual score on larger than oneself SAW needs would tend to have a high Organizational continuance commitment score and vice versa. The r squared indicates that 3.5% of the variance in Organizational continuance commitment scores can be predicted from the individual's score on larger than oneself component of SAW needs.]

H2.3a: Individual scores on Integrity and Wholeness component of Spirituality at Work would be positively related to Organizational normative commitment. [Supported. Significant positive relationship as per Pearson r correlation coefficient (r=0.417, p<.01, N=169) The positive coefficient indicates that the individuals having a high individual score on integrity and wholeness SAW needs would tend to have a high Organizational normative commitment score and vice versa. The r squared indicates that 17.4% of the variance in

Organizational normative commitment scores can be predicted from the individual's score on integrity and wholeness component of SAW needs.]

H2.3b: Individual scores on Meaningful work component of Spirituality at Work would be positively related to Organizational normative commitment. [Supported. Significant positive relationship as per Pearson r correlation coefficient (r=0.417, p<.01, N=169) The positive coefficient indicates that the individuals having a high individual score on meaningful work SAW needs would tend to have a high Organizational normative commitment score and vice versa. The r squared indicates that 17.4% of the variance in Organizational normative commitment scores can be predicted from the individual's score on meaningful work component of SAW needs.]

H2.3c: Individual scores on Larger than oneself component of Spirituality at Work would be positively related to Organizational normative commitment. [Supported. Significant positive relationship as per Pearson r correlation coefficient (r=0.454, p<.01, N=169) The positive coefficient indicates that the individuals having a high individual score on larger than oneself SAW needs would tend to have a high Organizational normative commitment score and vice versa. The r squared indicates that 20.6% of the variance in Organizational normative commitment scores can be predicted from the individual's score on larger than oneself component of SAW needs.]

H2.3d: Composite Individual scores on Spirituality at Work would be positively related to Organizational normative commitment. [Supported. Significant positive relationship as per Pearson r correlation coefficient (r=0.479, p<.01, N=169) The positive coefficient indicates that the individuals having a high individual composite SAW needs score would tend to have a high Organizational normative commitment score and vice versa. The r squared indicates that 22.9% of the variance in Organizational normative commitment scores can be predicted from the individual's composite SAW needs score.]

5.2.3.2 Organization-based set of hypotheses

Given the extant arguments in literature that highlight the organizational SAW supplies and their influence on outcomes, a number of organization-based hypotheses too were tested in this study. The corresponding correlation matrix is presented in Table 5.7 (Results are provided in parentheses).

	Mean	Std. Dev.	OC_A	OC_C	OC_N	JS
O_iw	3.7524	0.59573	.672(**)	-0.084	.462(**)	.767(**)
O_mw	4.0295	0.54442	.615(**)	0.027	.496(**)	.640(**)
O_lto	4.0791	0.57952	.582(**)	0.053	.455(**)	.699(**)
O_SAW	3.9534	0.51477	.693(**)	-0.003	.524(**)	.783(**)
OC_A	4.1858	0.69679	1	-0.002	.532(**)	.595(**)
OC_C	3.3598	0.54754		1	.192(*)	-0.013
OC_N	4.0343	0.66869			1	.508(**)
JS	3.6883	0.55625				1

** Correlation is significant at the 0.01 level (2-tailed).
* Correlation is significant at the 0.05 level (2-tailed).
Table 5.7 Correlation matrix for organization-based hypotheses

H3a: Scores on Integrity/Wholeness component of SAW supplies would be positively related to Job satisfaction. [Supported. Significant positive relationship as per Pearson r correlation coefficient (r=0.767, p<.01, N=169) The positive coefficient indicates that the individuals' perceptions of their organization having a high score on integrity and wholeness component of SAW supplies would tend to have a high job satisfaction score and vice versa. The r-squared indicates that approximately 58.8% of the variance in job satisfaction scores can be predicted from the individual's score on integrity and wholeness SAW supplies.]

H3b: Scores on Meaningful work component of SAW supplies would be positively related to Job satisfaction. [Supported. Significant positive relationship as per Pearson r correlation coefficient (r=0.640, p<.01, N=169) The positive coefficient indicates that the individuals' perceptions of their organization having a high score on meaningful work component of SAW supplies would tend to have a high job satisfaction score and vice versa. The r-squared indicates that approximately 40.1% of the variance in job satisfaction scores can be predicted from the individual's score on meaningful work SAW supplies.]

H3c: Scores on Larger than oneself component of SAW supplies would be positively related to Job satisfaction. [Supported. Significant positive relationship as per Pearson r correlation coefficient (r=0.699, p<.01, N=169). The positive coefficient indicates that the individuals' perceptions of their organization having a high score on larger than oneself component of SAW supplies would tend to have a high job satisfaction score and vice versa. The r-squared indicates that approximately 48.9% of the variance in job satisfaction scores can be predicted from the individual's score on larger than oneself SAW supplies.]

H3d: Composite scores on organizational SAW supplies would be positively related to Job satisfaction. [Supported. Significant positive relationship as per Pearson r correlation coefficient (r=0.783, p<.01, N=169) The positive coefficient indicates that the individuals' perceptions of a high score on Organizational SAW supplies would tend to have a high job satisfaction score and vice versa. The r-squared indicates that approximately 61.3% of the variance in job satisfaction scores can be predicted from the individual's composite score SAW supplies.]

H4.1a: Scores on Integrity and Wholeness component of SAW supplies would be positively related to Organizational affective commitment. [Supported. Significant positive relationship as per Pearson r correlation coefficient (r=0.672, p<.01, N=169) The positive coefficient indicates that the individuals' perceptions of a high Organizational score on integrity and wholeness SAW supplies would tend to have a high Organizational affective commitment score and vice versa. The r-squared indicates that approximately 45.15% of the variance in Organizational affective commitment scores can be predicted from the individual's score on integrity and wholeness component of SAW supplies.]

H4.1b: Scores on Meaningful work component of SAW supplies would be positively related to Organizational affective commitment. [Supported. Significant positive relationship as per Pearson r correlation coefficient (r=0.615, p<.01, N=169) The positive coefficient indicates that the individuals' perceptions of a high score on meaningful work component of SAW supplies would tend to have a high Organizational affective commitment score and vice versa. The r-squared indicates that approximately 37.82% of the variance in Organizational affective commitment scores can be predicted from the individual's score on meaningful work component of SAW supplies.]

H4.1c: Scores on Larger than oneself component of SAW supplies would be positively related to Organizational affective commitment. [Supported. Significant positive relationship as per Pearson r correlation coefficient (r=0.582, p<.01, N=169) The positive coefficient indicates that the individuals' perceptions of a high score on larger than oneself SAW supplies would tend to have a high Organizational affective commitment score and vice versa. The r-squared indicates that approximately 33.87% of the variance in Organizational affective commitment scores can be predicted from the individual's score on larger than oneself component of SAW supplies.]

H4.1d: Composite scores on SAW supplies would be positively related to Organizational affective commitment. [Supported. Significant positive relationship as per Pearson r correlation coefficient (r=0.693, p<.01, N=169) The positive coefficient indicates that the individuals' perceptions of a high score on SAW supplies would tend to have a high Organizational affective commitment score and vice versa. The r-squared indicates that approximately 48% of the variance in Organizational affective commitment scores can be predicted from the individual's composite score on SAW supplies.]

H4.2a: Scores on Integrity and Wholeness component of SAW supplies would be positively related to Organizational continuance commitment. [Not supported. Insignificant negative relationship as per Pearson r correlation coefficient (r=-.084, p<.278, N=169) The negative coefficient indicates that the individuals' perceptions of a high score on integrity and wholeness SAW supplies would tend to have a low Organizational continuance commitment score and vice versa. The r-squared indicates that less than 0.7% of the variance in Organizational continuance commitment scores can be predicted from the individual's score on integrity and wholeness component of SAW supplies.]

H4.2b: Scores on Meaningful work component of SAW supplies would be positively related to Organizational continuance commitment. [Not supported. Insignificant positive relationship as per Pearson r correlation coefficient ($r=0.080$, $p<.303$, $N=169$) The positive coefficient indicates that the individuals' perceptions of a high score on meaningful work SAW supplies would tend to have a high Organizational continuance commitment score and vice versa. The r-squared indicates that slightly higher than 0.6% of the variance in Organizational continuance commitment scores can be predicted from the individual's score on meaningful work component of SAW supplies.]

H4.2c: Scores on Larger than oneself component of SAW supplies would be positively related to Organizational continuance commitment. [Not supported. Insignificant positive relationship as per Pearson r correlation coefficient ($r=0.027$, $p<.725$, $N=169$) The positive coefficient indicates that the individuals' perceptions of a high score on larger than oneself SAW supplies would tend to have a high Organizational continuance commitment score and vice versa. The r-squared indicates that 1% of the variance in Organizational continuance commitment scores can be predicted from the individual's score on larger than oneself component of SAW supplies.]

H4.2d: Composite scores on SAW supplies would be positively related to Organizational continuance commitment. [Not supported. Insignificant negative relationship as per Pearson r correlation coefficient ($r=-0.003$, $p<.968$, $N=169$) The negative coefficient indicates that the individuals' perceptions of a high score on larger than oneself SAW supplies would tend to have a low Organizational continuance commitment score and vice versa. The r-squared indicates that 0.001% of the variance in Organizational continuance commitment scores can be predicted from the individual's score on larger than oneself component of SAW supplies.]

H4.3a: Scores on Integrity and Wholeness component of SAW supplies would be positively related to Organizational normative commitment. [Supported. Significant positive relationship as per Pearson r correlation coefficient ($r=0.462$, $p<.01$, $N=169$) The positive coefficient indicates that the Individuals' perceptions of a high score on integrity and wholeness SAW supplies would tend to have a high Organizational normative commitment score and vice versa. The r-squared indicates that 21.34% of the variance in Organizational normative commitment scores can be predicted from the individual's score on integrity and wholeness component of SAW supplies.]

H4.3b: Scores on Meaningful work component of SAW supplies would be positively related to Organizational normative commitment. [Supported. Significant positive relationship as per

Pearson r correlation coefficient (r=0.496, p<.01, N=169) The positive coefficient indicates that the individuals' perceptions of a high score on meaningful work SAW supplies would tend to have a high Organizational normative commitment score and vice versa. The r-squared indicates that 24.6% of the variance in Organizational normative commitment scores can be predicted from the individual's score on meaningful work component of SAW supplies.]

H4.3c: Scores on Larger than oneself component of Spirituality at Work would be positively related to Organizational normative commitment. [Supported. Significant positive relationship as per Pearson r correlation coefficient (r=0.455, p<.01, N=169) The positive coefficient indicates that the individuals' perceptions of a high score on larger than oneself SAW supplies would tend to have a high Organizational normative commitment score and vice versa. The r-squared indicates that 20.7% of the variance in Organizational normative commitment scores can be predicted from the individual's score on larger than oneself component of SAW supplies.]

H4.3d: Composite scores on SAW supplies would be positively related to Organizational normative commitment. [Supported. Significant positive relationship as per Pearson r correlation coefficient (r=0.524, p<.01, N=169) The positive coefficient indicates that the individuals' perceptions of a high score on composite SAW supplies would tend to have a high Organizational normative commitment score and vice versa. The r-squared indicates that 27.46% of the variance in Organizational normative commitment scores can be predicted from the individual's composite score on SAW supplies.]

5.2.3.3 Person-organization fit based set of hypotheses

Given that this study had argued for the utilization of the P-O fit perspective to examine SAW and its consequences, a number of related hypotheses were tested. The corresponding correlation matrix is presented below in Table 5.8.

	Mean	Std. Dev.	OC_A	OC_C	OC_N	JS
Iwdiff	0.3762	0.50065	-.364(**)	.169(*)	-0.141	-.495(**)
Mwdiff	0.3734	0.42128	-.329(**)	0.047	-.161(*)	-.334(**)
LTOdiff	0.4262	0.52257	-.406(**)	0.085	-.234(**)	-.503(**)
SAWdiff	0.3925	0.39543	-.448(**)	0.126	-.220(**)	-.549(**)
OC_A	4.1858	0.69679	1	-0.002	.532(**)	.595(**)
OC_C	3.3598	0.54754		1	.192(*)	-0.013
OC_N	4.0343	0.66869			1	.508(**)
JS	3.6883	0.55625				1

** Correlation is significant at the 0.01 level (2-tailed).
* Correlation is significant at the 0.05 level (2-tailed).

Table 5.8 Correlation matrix for person-organization fit based hypotheses

Iwdiff = score of Individual needs on integrity and wholeness less score on organizational supplies of integrity and wholeness = [$I_{iw} - O_{iw}$]

Mwdiff = score of Individual needs on meaningful work less score on organizational supplies of meaningful work = $[I_{mw} - O_{mw}]$

Iwdiff = score of Individual needs on larger than oneself less score on organizational supplies of larger than oneself = $[I_{lto} - O_{lto}]$

SAWdiff = score of composite individual SAW needs less score of composite organizational SAW supplies = $[I_{saw} - O_{saw}]$

It should be noted that in Table 5.8 negative correlation scores for the three difference scores would indicate that the greater the divergence between individual needs and organizational SAW supplies the lesser would be the desired score on outcome variables. Hypothesis-wise details are provided below (Results being provided in parentheses):

H5a: P-O fit scores on Integrity/Wholeness component of Spirituality at Work would be negatively related to Job satisfaction. [Supported. Significant negative relationship as per Pearson r correlation coefficient ($r=-0.495$, $p<.01$, N=169) The negative coefficient indicates that the individuals having a high score on integrity and wholeness component of SAW P-O fit would tend to have a low job satisfaction score and vice versa. The r-squared indicates that approximately 24.5% of the variance in job satisfaction scores can be predicted from the individual's score on integrity and wholeness component of SAW P-O fit.]

H5b: P-O fit scores on Meaningful work component of Spirituality at Work would be negatively related to Job satisfaction. [Supported. Significant negative relationship as per Pearson r correlation coefficient ($r=-0.334$, $p<.01$, N=169) The negative coefficient indicates that the individuals having a high score on meaningful work component of SAW P-O fit would tend to have a low job satisfaction score and vice versa. The r-squared indicates that approximately 11.1% of the variance in job satisfaction scores can be predicted from the individual's score on meaningful work component of SAW P-O fit.]

H5c: P-O fit scores on Larger than oneself component of Spirituality at Work would be negatively related to Job satisfaction. [Supported. Significant negative relationship as per Pearson r correlation coefficient ($r=-0.503$, $p<.01$, N=169) The negative coefficient indicates that the individuals having a high score on larger than oneself component of SAW P-O fit would tend to have a low job satisfaction score and vice versa. The r-squared indicates that approximately 25.3% of the variance in job satisfaction scores can be predicted from the individual's score on larger than oneself component of SAW P-O fit.]

H5d: Composite P-O fit scores on Spirituality at Work would be negatively related to Job satisfaction. [Supported. Significant negative relationship as per Pearson r correlation coefficient ($r=-0.549$, $p<.01$, N=169) The negative coefficient indicates that the individuals having a high score on individual component of SAW P-O fit would tend to have a low job satisfaction score and vice versa. The r-squared indicates that approximately 30.14% of the variance in job satisfaction scores can be predicted from the individual's composite score component of SAW P-O fit.]

H6.1a: P-O fit scores on Integrity/Wholeness component of Spirituality at Work would be negatively related to Organizational affective commitment. [Supported. Significant negative relationship as per Pearson r correlation coefficient (r=-0.364, p<.01, N=169) The negative coefficient indicates that the individuals having a high individual score on integrity and wholeness SAW need would tend to have a low Organizational affective commitment score and vice versa. The r-squared indicates that approximately 13.25% of the variance in Organizational affective commitment scores can be predicted from the individual's score on integrity and wholeness component of SAW P-O fit.]

H6.1b: P-O fit scores on Meaningful work component of Spirituality at Work would be negatively related to Organizational affective commitment. [Supported. Significant negative relationship as per Pearson r correlation coefficient (r=-0.329, p<.01, N=169) The negative coefficient indicates that the individuals having a high individual score on meaningful work component of SAW P-O fit would tend to have a low Organizational affective commitment score and vice versa. The r-squared indicates that approximately 10.82% of the variance in Organizational affective commitment scores can be predicted from the individual's score on meaningful work component of SAW P-O fit.]

H6.1c: P-O fit scores on Larger than oneself component of Spirituality at Work would be negatively related to Organizational affective commitment. [Supported. Significant negative relationship as per Pearson r correlation coefficient (r=-0.406, p<.01, N=169) The negative coefficient indicates that the individuals having a high individual score on larger than oneself component of SAW P-O fit would tend to have a low Organizational affective commitment score and vice versa. The r-squared indicates that approximately 16.48% of the variance in Organizational affective commitment scores can be predicted from the individual's score on larger than oneself component of SAW P-O fit.]

H6.1d: Composite P-O fit scores on Spirituality at Work would be negatively related to Organizational affective commitment. [Supported. Significant negative relationship as per Pearson r correlation coefficient (r=-0.448, p<.01, N=169) The negative coefficient indicates that the individuals having a high composite SAW P-O fit score would tend to have a high Organizational affective commitment score and vice versa. The r-squared indicates that approximately 20.1% of the variance in Organizational affective commitment scores can be predicted from the individual's composite score on SAW P-O fit.]

H6.2a: P-O fit scores on Integrity and Wholeness component of Spirituality at Work would be negatively related to Organizational continuance commitment. [Not supported. Significant positive relationship as per Pearson r correlation coefficient (r=0.169, p<.028, N=169) The positive coefficient indicates that the individuals having a high score on integrity and wholeness component of SAW P-O fit would tend to have a high Organizational continuance commitment score and vice versa. The r-squared indicates that less than 2.85% of the variance in Organizational continuance commitment scores can be predicted from the score on integrity and wholeness component of SAW P-O fit.]

H6.2b: P-O fit scores on Meaningful work component of Spirituality at Work would be negatively related to Organizational continuance commitment. [Not supported. Insignificant positive relationship as per Pearson r correlation coefficient ($r=0.047$, $p<.303$, $N=169$) The positive coefficient indicates that the individuals having a high score on meaningful work component of SAW P-O fit would tend to have a high Organizational continuance commitment score and vice versa. The r-squared indicates that slightly higher than 2% of the variance in Organizational continuance commitment scores can be predicted from the score on meaningful work component of SAW P-O fit.]

H6.2c: P-O fit scores on Larger than oneself component of Spirituality at Work would be negatively related to Organizational continuance commitment. [Not supported. Significant positive relationship as per Pearson r correlation coefficient ($r=0.085$, $p<.015$, $N=169$) The positive coefficient indicates that the individuals having a high score on larger than oneself component of SAW P-O fit would tend to have a high Organizational continuance commitment score and vice versa. The r-squared indicates that 0.7% of the variance in Organizational continuance commitment scores can be predicted from the score on larger than oneself component of SAW P-O fit.]

H6.2d: Composite P-O fit scores on Spirituality at Work would be negatively related to Organizational continuance commitment. [Not supported. Insignificant positive relationship as per Pearson r correlation coefficient ($r=0.126$, $p<.1015$, $N=169$) The positive coefficient indicates that the individuals having a high score on larger than oneself component of SAW P-O fit would tend to have a high Organizational continuance commitment score and vice versa. The r-squared indicates that 3.5% of the variance in Organizational continuance commitment scores can be predicted from the score on larger than oneself component of component of SAW P-O fit.]

H6.3a: P-O fit scores on Integrity and Wholeness component of Spirituality at Work would be negatively related to Organizational normative commitment. [Supported weakly. Insignificant negative relationship as per Pearson r correlation coefficient ($r=-0.141$, $p<.068$, $N=169$) The negative coefficient indicates that the individuals having a high score on integrity and wholeness component of SAW P-O fit would tend to have a low Organizational normative commitment score and vice versa. The r-squared indicates that slightly less than 2% of the variance in Organizational normative commitment scores can be predicted from the score on integrity and wholeness component of SAW P-O fit.]

H6.3b: P-O fit scores on Meaningful work component of Spirituality at Work would be negatively related to Organizational normative commitment. [Supported. Significant negative relationship as per Pearson r correlation coefficient ($r=-0.161$, $p<.05$, $N=169$) The negative coefficient indicates that the individuals having a high individual score on meaningful work component of SAW P-O fit would tend to have a low Organizational normative commitment score and vice versa. The r-squared indicates that 2.6% of the variance in Organizational normative commitment scores can be predicted from the score on meaningful work component of SAW P-O fit.]

H6.3c: P-O fit scores on Larger than oneself component of Spirituality at Work would be negatively related to Organizational normative commitment. [Supported. Significant negative relationship as per Pearson r correlation coefficient (r=-0.234, p<.01, N=169) The negative coefficient indicates that the individuals having a high individual score on larger than oneself component of SAW P-O fit would tend to have a low Organizational normative commitment score and vice versa. The r-squared indicates that 5.5% of the variance in Organizational normative commitment scores can be predicted from the score on larger than oneself component of SAW P-O fit.]

H6.3d: Composite P-O fit scores on Spirituality at Work would be negatively related to Organizational normative commitment. [Supported. Significant negative relationship as per Pearson r correlation coefficient (r=-0.220, p<.01, N=169) The negative coefficient indicates that the individuals having a high individual composite component of SAW P-O fit score would tend to have a high Organizational normative commitment score and vice versa. The r-squared indicates that 4.84% of the variance in Organizational normative commitment scores can be predicted from the individual's composite SAW P-O fit score.]

Separate partial correlation matrices were also computed to control for the effects of various demographic variables – Age group, Educational qualifications, Tenure in organizations, and Sex – but no appreciable differences could be discerned in the correlation scores.

Hypotheses supported		Job Satisfaction	Affective organizational commitment	Continuance organizational commitment	Normative organizational commitment
Integrity and wholeness	Individual needs	Supported	Supported	Not supported	Supported
	Organizational supplies	Supported	Supported	Not supported	Supported
	P-O fit	Supported	Supported	Not supported	Supported
Meaningful Work	Individual needs	Supported	Supported	Not supported	Supported
	Organizational supplies	Supported	Supported	Not supported	Supported
	P-O fit	Supported	Supported	Not supported	Supported
Larger than oneself	Individual needs	Supported	Supported	Supported	Supported
	Organizational supplies	Supported	Supported	Not supported	Supported
	P-O fit	Supported	Supported	Not supported	Supported
Composite SAW score	Individual needs	Supported	Supported	Not supported	Supported
	Organizational supplies	Supported	Supported	Not supported	Supported
	P-O fit	Supported	Supported	Not supported	Supported

Table 5.9: Summary of Correlation Table Results

Summarizing the above, it can be observed that except for the correlations for organizational continuance commitment, those for the other outcome variables validate the hypotheses of this study. The corresponding values for outcome variables on the sub-scale and scale-level independent variables were both positive and highly significant at 0.01 level (2-tailed) indicating that a higher individual need for SAW – and a higher perceived organizational SAW supply – was likely to have a higher score on job satisfaction, organizational affective commitment and organizational normative commitment.

Overall, it can be observed from this section that but for the scores for organizational continuance commitment on which the evidence was rather equivocal, hypotheses related to the other outcome variables were largely supported. However, it can be seen that organizational SAW supplies are more strongly correlated to the outcome variables than are individual SAW needs. Further, correlation scores on organizational SAW are also better than those for the various SAW P-O fit scores. Implications of these findings shall be discussed in the next chapter.

5.2.4 Regression analysis results

Hierarchical regression analysis was conducted to examine the impact of various demographics variables on the prediction of the outcome variables from a combination of independent variables. Four such regressions were conducted to determine the best linear combinations of P-O fit on SAW, individual SAW needs and organizational SAW supplies that help predict job satisfaction, organizational affective commitment, organizational continuance commitment, and organizational normative commitment respectively.

For all the hierarchical regression analyses, Age group ID, Educational group ID, years in organization ID, and sex were entered in a hierarchical fashion to investigate the change in variance explained due to their introduction. The hierarchical regression analysis was replicated repeatedly by trying out different orders of introducing these variables but it led to no appreciable difference in variance explained.

For all the four regression equations that were generated, the variable relating to organizational SAW supplies was excluded indicating that individual SAW needs score along with the P-O fit score variables were sufficient to predict the various outcome variables. [Further, since the P-O fit score was an arithmetical derivation of the individual SAW needs and organizational SAW supplies scores, the omission of either the individual SAW needs or the organizational SAW supplies is not surprising.] Subsequently, the same analysis was repeated without including the individual SAW needs variable but the variance explained differed by only 0.1%. It can thus be concluded that either of individual SAW needs or organizational SAW supplies can be used to predict the various outcome variables though the predictions would improve only marginally by using individual SAW needs variable instead of the organizational SAW supplies.

A representative model summary for Job Satisfaction is provided in Table 5.10 below:

					Change Statistics				
Model	R	R Square	Adjusted R Square	Std. Error of the Estimate	R Square Change	F Change	df1	df2	Sig. F Change
1	.783ª	.614	.609	.34781	.614	131.852	2	166	.000
2	.785ᵇ	.616	.609	.34797	.002	.845	1	165	.359
3	.785ᶜ	.616	.607	.34885	.000	.172	1	164	.679
4	.786ᵈ	.618	.606	.34903	.002	.832	1	163	.363
5	.786ᵉ	.618	.604	.35010	.000	.001	1	162	.970

Model Summary[f]

a. Predictors: (Constant), I_SAW, SAWdiff
b. Predictors: (Constant), I_SAW, SAWdiff, AgeGrpID
c. Predictors: (Constant), I_SAW, SAWdiff, AgeGrpID, EduGpID
d. Predictors: (Constant), I_SAW, SAWdiff, AgeGrpID, EduGpID, yrsOrgnID
e. Predictors: (Constant), I_SAW, SAWdiff, AgeGrpID, EduGpID, yrsOrgnID, Sex
f. Dependent Variable: JS

Table 5.10: Hierarchical Regression analysis summary for job satisfaction

It can be seen from the model summary above that 60.9% of the variance in job satisfaction can be predicted from the independent variables of individual SAW needs and SAW P-O fit scores. Further, the coefficients of the model with their respective t-values and significance revealed that only the individual SAW needs and scores on SAW P-O fit contributed significantly to the final equation. The Beta weights, presented in Table 5.11, suggest that individual SAW needs contribute positively to predicting job satisfaction, and SAW difference scores (indicating the lack of P-O fit) contribute negatively to the prediction.

Variable	B	SEB	ß
Individual SAW needs	0.803	0.077	.553**
SAW difference score	-0.867	0.070	-0.616**
Age group	0.040	0.033	0.076
Education group	-0.012	0.025	-0.025
Years in organization	-0.023	0.027	-0.055

Note: $R^2 = 0.604$; $F(6, 162) = 43.683$, $p<0.000$

Table 5.11: Beta weights in the regression equation

The results for organizational affective commitment and organizational normative commitment were largely similar with the same combination of variables as above explaining 48.8% and 34.1% of the variance in predicted variables respectively.

However, the model for organizational continuance commitment proved to be unsatisfactory with the final model involving all predictor variables explaining only 6.5% of the variance of outcome variable.

5.2.5 Analysis of organizational differences with ANOVA

A comparison of the two categories of organizations on various parameters was attempted with ANOVA. The results are presented in Table 5.12.

		Sum of Squares	df	Mean Square	F	Sig.
I_SAW	Between Groups	1.743	1	1.743	12.711	0.000
	Within Groups	22.903	167	0.137		
	Total	24.647	168			
O_SAW	Between Groups	8.600	1	8.600	39.984	0.000
	Within Groups	35.918	167	0.215		
	Total	44.518	168			
OC_A	Between Groups	22.080	1	22.080	61.986	0.000
	Within Groups	59.486	167	0.356		
	Total	81.566	168			
OC_C	Between Groups	0.211	1	0.211	0.702	0.403
	Within Groups	50.155	167	0.300		
	Total	50.366	168			
OC_N	Between Groups	7.797	1	7.797	19.340	0.000
	Within Groups	67.324	167	0.403		
	Total	75.121	168			
JS	Between Groups	4.085	1	4.085	14.242	0.000
	Within Groups	47.898	167	0.287		
	Total	51.982	168			

The F tests the effect of O_Type.
This test is based on the linearly independent pairwise comparisons among the estimated marginal means.
Table 5.12: ANOVA Table for O_Type

The results indicate that the two categories differed not only in the perceptions about availability of SAW supplies but even in terms of SAW needs at individual level. What this finding indicates is that not only do the two categories differ in terms of the organizational availability of SAW supplies but also in terms of SAW needs of the individuals who work in them. Further, the two types of organizations differed on all outcome variables except the continuance organizational commitment.

While Table 5.12 demonstrates that organizations differed based on their being explicitly spiritual or explicitly non-spiritual, follow-up post-hoc test (Tukey HSD) on organization i-d indicated that they did not fall into neat homogeneous sub-sets on that classification. A representative set of tables for organizational SAW supplies, affective organizational commitment, and normative organizational commitment are provided below.

Tukey HSD [a, b]

OrgnID	N	Subset for alpha = .05		
		1	2	3
1	29	3.5690		
2	29	3.6134		
5	34		3.9774	
3	21		4.0481	
6	31		4.0603	
4	25			4.5492
Sig.		0.999	0.975	1.000

Means for groups in homogeneous subsets are displayed.
a. Uses Harmonic Mean Sample Size = 27.491.
b. The group sizes are unequal. The harmonic mean of the group sizes is used. Type I error levels are not guaranteed.

Table 5.13: Tukey HSD for homogeneous sub-sets of organizations on organizational SAW supplies scores

OrgnID	N	Subset for alpha = .05				
		1	2	3	4	5
1	29	3.5931				
2	29	3.8276	3.8276			
3	21		4.0476	4.0476		
5	34			4.3353	4.3353	
6	31				4.5161	4.5161
4	25					4.7920
Sig.		0.657	0.716	0.434	0.852	0.483

Table 5.14: Tukey HSD for homogeneous sub-sets of organizations on affective organizational commitment scores

OrgnID	N	Subset for alpha = .05		
		1	2	3
1	29	3.7034		
2	29	3.7517		
5	34	3.9706	3.9706	
3	21	4.0190	4.0190	
6	31		4.2452	4.2452
4	25			4.5840
Sig.		0.394	0.553	0.313

Table 5.15: Tukey HSD for homogeneous sub-sets of organizations on normative organizational commitment scores

The post-hoc tests – which fail to discriminate neatly between two kinds of organizations - thus indicate that organizations can not be classified into explicitly-spiritual and explicitly non-spiritual category and that instead it may be useful to think of organizations as lying on a continuum of available opportunity structures for spiritual expression and manifestation. However, it may be noted that regardless of the organizations not falling neatly into two categories they still largely adhere to their order of grouping into the explicitly-spiritual (organizations 4, 5, 6) and not-explicitly-spiritual (organizations 1, 2, 3)

Implications of the results above shall be discussed in the discussions and conclusions chapter.

5.3 Qualitative data analysis results

As was mentioned in the methodology chapter, this study utilized both quantitative and qualitative data collection techniques to answer the research questions. In particular, interview data was collected to explore the issues relating to: the sources of interest in SAW, how SAW is understood in an organizational context, the ways SAW manifests in an organizational context, and the influence of the organizational context in expression of SAW. To begin with, the researcher sought to test the utility of Mitroff and Denton's workplace spirituality instrument for collecting data from 39 corporate executives who come for Management Development Programs on IIM-C campus. It was soon apparent that the corporate executives had a difficult time in accessing issues related to spirituality and its expression in the workplace. Mitroff and Denton's fears of the difficulty in accessing SAW issues in the corporate set-up (Mitroff & Denton, 1999a) were thus confronted in this study too.

The distinction between the corporate executives and the respondents in the non-profit sector became obvious when data was collected form the nonprofits later. The relative readiness of the latter to engage in issues relating to SAW was at once noticeable. Not only was the readiness seen amongst the respondents from the explicitly-spiritual organizations but even amongst the other non-profits the larger than oneself theme of SAW was easily accessible. These observations vindicated the stand of this study that the non-profit sector may provide more appropriate settings to access and assess issues relating to SAW. Beyond these overall impressions about the interviews and the relative ease with which SAW issues could be explored in the selected sector, responses to the various questions that were raised shall be provided below.

5.3.1 Factors prompting engagement with SAW

A majority of our respondents related their desire for engaging with spirituality to their personal relationships with close family members, friends and others from the early years of their lives. Family upbringing in an environment conducive to generating an interest in such issues emerged as a strong influence in prompting this study's respondents to grapple with spirituality. The same influence also led them later to search for an appropriate working place where such aspirations would be respected. One representative sampling from such responses was:

> I was brought up in an environment where both my parents were initiated by the third President of Ramakrishna Mission. As such the environment at home was almost like that of the RKM itself. We would have the sandhya-vandana including the Sri Ramakrishna aratikam every evening. It did not matter to them that I may have an exam next day and may just not have prepared for it. If it was time for the arati, it was time for the arati. Similarly, in the night time there was this curious practice of reading scriptures. Each child would be given the opportunity to read aloud from a suitable text and explain it to others. The monks of the RKM and similar other institutions were continuously invited to our house. Even later when I went

away for my advanced studies, the same strain continued and I remained dedicated to the philosophy. Now with that frame of mind one could not have joined any other organization. Not surprisingly perhaps, when it was the time to look for a job I decided to look for a place that resonated with a similar spiritual aim and came to SAIC. Now, the thought of leaving this institute itself bothers me.

A few others attributed organizational ideology as a major factor prompting their search for spirituality. This organizational influence though does not necessarily begin only after joining a particular organization but exerts its impact even from early informal contacts. In particular, the influence exerted by certain charismatic individuals during these encounters proved to be decisive for a few of this study's respondents. One such respondent recounted that experience:

My mother had been in close touch with the Aurobindo Ashram at Pondicherry and used to visit it annually. I remember that there was a thin book that used to be there in our house from the Aurobindo mission. [On being asked about a decisive event that inspired him] No single event really... that probably happened later... a decisive event that would lay the foundation of my life-long association with the Aurobindo Ashram.

It was January 1970 and my mother was planning her second visit to Pondicherry. I was rather attached to my mother and did not want to get left out. I was convinced that I should accompany my mother to Pondicherry. My mother thought that I was being very unreasonable but my father agreed with me. We went there by a flight and I remember all the details of that flight. Not that I was flying for the first time but I remember the clouds along the way and an impeccably maintained campus once we landed in Pondicherry. I guess I remember all that because of the level of anticipation that I had of the trip.

I remember waiting that morning for the darshan and then we moved in to The Mother's room and I remember the first sight of a very old looking lady. The boy who entered and the person who emerged from that room that day were two very different people. I do not know what happened in that meeting but after that one instance I wanted to go to Pondicherry every time and explore the mystique of that frail lady there.

The impression that I carry from that experience is that I decided that all that I wanted to know in life was the mystique of that old lady and nothing else... Everything in life would be cast aside for that one person. Everything then began to orient itself towards knowing The Mother... everything became an exercise in knowing her better. With passing years maybe I am coming closer to that... I feel that my destiny is intertwined with that of the ashrama... [Speaking of one's current role in the organization] When I came here I thought that probably I was necessary for the place. However, today I feel that this work was necessary for me. Today I feel that when I leave this place I might leave it worse off than the shape in which I had found it. I feel that I do not control the work. I believe very fundamentally, from deep inside me, that it is Her work!

Beyond one's upbringing and the personal contact with certain charismatic individuals, another factor that was important – though for a fewer number of respondents - was the spiritually disengaging experiences in earlier organizations. They then sought solace in organizations and activities where they would feel more involved and be engaged in more meaningful roles. One such respondent recollected his earlier experience in healthcare institutions:

After my post-graduate degree in business management I entered the workforce and served a number of hospitals one after the other. Essentially the task was to solicit general physicians and motivate them to refer their patients to our hospital for treatment. These doctors would be offered a commission based on their referrals and I detested the job that I was doing: it was all profiting from someone else's misery. The doctor who forwarded the patient to us would get a commission based on the patient's bill and the hospital too would try to fleece the patient to the maximum extent possible. Besides, all that I was doing was so very repetitive: one doctor was just the same as any other!

Although I had never thought that I'll get into the non-profit sector but being in marketing I realized that this sector, which contributes such a lot to the society, too needed some marketing orientation... Obviously, the change in orientation would not be in terms of profiting from others' misery but in terms of making these non-profits more responsive to the needs of the community and also making the community aware of the role being played by the non-profit organizations themselves. My skills could be put to much better and socially responsible use here, I thought...

Upon joining here I realized that the organizational goals were much broader and that the same attitude pervaded throughout the organization. The environment was more relaxed and there was much scope for learning... In the earlier organization the only concern was about surpassing targets: I routinely did it myself and imposed it on my subordinates as well... That way there was a sea-change in the environment from where I was working to where I had come... I could take things at my own pace...

Another issue that was important for still fewer respondents was that of balancing the increasingly materialistic outlook in society. Driven by a concern for a society populated only by self-seeking individuals, they sought to counter it with their own involvement in self-less activities.

5.3.2 Understanding of SAW inside organizations

One major issue for this study was enquiring into the understanding of SAW in organizations and enriching the academic literature that presently converges towards three central SAW themes: integrity and wholeness, meaningful work, and larger than oneself. While the survey instrument gathered the views of respondents on their SAW needs and organizational supplies on these three themes, the open-ended question on the issue was expected to elicit respondents' understanding of spirituality. It was also hoped that the open-ended query would help assess if respondents of the two organization types – explicitly-spiritual and otherwise – differ significantly in their conception and usage of the term.

The themes identified from academic literature were validated from the responses that were received. The ability to be one whole in the workplace (indicative of the integrity and wholeness theme), the desire for the work resonating with one's sense of purpose and meaningfulness, and that of contributing positively to one's environment were repeatedly encountered across most cases. Nonetheless, there were other SAW themes that could not be captured directly under these three headings alone.

A central characteristic of the dimension not captured in the extant SAW themes was the importance of one's attitude towards the work that one was engaged in. The attitude of surrender to a higher power has been mentioned earlier. An associated attitude was one of cultivated detachment: unattached action with the focus being completely on appropriate engagement with the present without spending excessive psychic energy on outcomes of one's actions and efforts. *Nishkama karma*, as it was termed by a sizeable section of the respondents, was considered the appropriate attitude of a spiritually-inclined individual towards the multifarious demands of the workplace.

Further, most respondents of this study did not agree with the traditionally accepted dichotomy between spiritual and material dimensions of life. While there indeed was a section of respondents who had come to a spiritual outlook to balance the increasing material focus in society, a majority agreed that a spiritual understanding of life would not mean only spiritual practices but would permeate all aspects of living. A representative response in this category is presented below:

> [Is spirituality relevant to the workplace?] They are actually indistinguishable. The more we separate spirituality from anything else then the problem arises. Our outlook should change, I feel. Earlier I also used to separate spirituality from work but now I do not. [What was your outlook earlier and what is it now?] Earlier I used to think that if I work more I would be sacrificing my practices and hampering my spiritual development... The idea was that focusing only on one's work shall lead to spiritual starvation. I used to be very strict about my spiritual practices therefore. But I think now that it is necessary to not be an extremist in either way! You should be neither too strict nor too liberal about your practices.
> [On being asked if spirituality could be practiced at work] The issue is that one should not separate one's spiritual self from the working self and realize that only talking about *shastras* is not practicing spirituality... working systematically would also be an expression of spirituality...

An overwhelming majority of the respondents of this study appeared to side with the point of view that spirituality was inextricably linked to its religious source. A tiny minority (4 out of 77 respondents who agreed to engage with this question) did feel that the religious undertones if applied to spirituality could only come at the cost of its universal nature.

However, beyond the considerations of religious underpinnings of spirituality a clear distinction amongst the two categories of respondent organizations was apparent in the emphasis on various themes relating to SAW. The emphasis in non-spiritual focus non-profits was decidedly on the communitarian aspects of spirituality and its contribution towards providing meaning to one's life. Respondents from explicitly-spiritual organizations, on the other hand, related their SAW understanding to the ideals of seeing one-ness with one and all and the attendant merging of ego in the Absolute. A representative respondent from an explicitly-spiritual organization spoke thus about it:

> Ten years ago, if you had asked me this question [What does the term spirituality mean to you?] I would have given you a very book-ish answer but my tenure here has helped me have clearer ideas about those words: God, Realization, Spiritual practice... My conception comes closest to what we call Advaita Vedanta... it is the idea of an Unbroken Undivided Existence which is also Consciousness (not passive) and "that" is the reality... not even the ultimate reality but also the only Reality there is... All the infinite manifestations that we see around us are like the waves in an ocean coming up and going down. In the last ten years, this has been transformed from something that I had read in the books and that had appealed to me... a certain intellectual understanding has since been converted into an intuitive grasp of its truth. All human beings, all living beings, all non-living beings, all seen and the unseen... they are all the manifestations of the One vibrant reality. In fact, the individual person, the person Biswarup [respondent's name] who thought that he was seeking ten years ago no longer exists... Am I making sense to you? Because if I am not then maybe the traditional pundits will agree that I am closer to the mark. [...laughs...]

Another idea that was central to the explicitly-spiritual organizational members' understanding of spirituality was the attendant attitude of surrender. In such organizations it was not unusual to find that the individual identity was surrendered at the altar of the Ideal!

A sample of the latter has been provided earlier in that extract where the respondent talks about feeling less egoistical about one's role in the organization and seeing it as having come for one's own good.

In contrast, the feature of selflessness and surrender was singularly absent from the lexicon of the respondents of the other non-profits. Feelings about spirituality and benefits from it too were more self-benefit driven in these non-profit organizations. Perhaps the difference lay in the reasons for which individual joined these organizations, motivated though they may have been with a feeling for the larger good. One such respondent remarked:

> Is it any surprise that our employees do not feel a sense of spiritual obligation towards the organization, the society and beyond? After all, they were recruited based on their qualifications and their rewards too are based on their individual professional attainments... Given that all the rewards and recognition are determined by the material contribution that one is making individually, expecting them to give up on their selfish motives and actions would really be asking for the moon.

The central distinction then between the two organizational categories appeared to be in the perception of outcomes of individual actions: whereas for the respondents from explicitly-spiritual organizations work was a means towards a transcendental end it remained largely humanitarian for the other non-profits. Implications of this distinction and the other perceptions about SAW shall be explored in the next chapter.

5.3.3 Manifestation of SAW inside organizations

Another major issue for examination in this study was how spirituality got manifested in an organizational context. For the reason that spirituality has been assumed to be a personal/individual affair, it was felt that a significant contribution could be made if organizational practices, routines, and principles of SAW manifestation could be isolated and compared across organizations.

The respondents were asked for their opinions on how spirituality could be expressed in an organizational context and for a list of specific behaviors and organizational features that could help or hinder its manifestation. Further, the respondents were also asked to relate instances that illustrated the practice of SAW in their organization.

From the 114 one-to-one interviews in which respondents were asked about how spirituality could be manifested in an organizational context, two broad directions of expression could be inferred: individual and organizational. Before discussing the organizational manifestation of spirituality, the individual category shall be elaborated on as it displayed an interesting divergence in emphasis.

At the individual level, the SAW expression issue could be sub-divided into being and doing streams. While it was the being aspect of individual spirituality that was emphasized in explicitly-spiritual organizations, the interviewees from other non-profits focused on the doing part. One typical response from an explicitly-spiritual organization was:

There could be two ways of looking at it. From the theoretical point of view, you cannot practice spirituality at work or anything like that. One becomes spiritual through realization or brahma-jnana and then expresses that realization in thought, word and deed. It is a rather private issue and can only be expressed to oneself... however, that is only one side of the picture. The other side could be that until one reaches the stage of brahma-jnana... what happens before that ? Until that time, one can use work as a means, as a sadhana that is where spirituality comes into work. We can see three stages in it, if we so wish:
i. Work "and" worship: where one still feels a real difference between so called secular works and so called spiritual pursuits. One would then work in the normal fashion and practice spiritual disciplines separately, as enjoined by the guru, scriptures or received instructions
ii. Work "as" worship: Practicing work unselfishly, that itself becomes a spiritual discipline. Spirituality and unselfish work then merge and become one.
iii. Work "is" worship: It is the ultimate stage of spirituality at work. It has almost become a cliché to say that work is worship but it has a very profound meaning for those in Advaita Vedanta in that it expresses the ultimate truth. It is only when you perceive everything as the one indivisible undivided reality then you can work. A work that would appear abominable to someone, to a brahma-jnani that work will appear to be worship.
This is how I view the connection between work and spirituality.

At a philosophical level, the being position of individual spirituality was justified with the following:

...an unshakeable intellectual conviction is required. the practice of jnana, bhakti, karma in your daily life. Prema for fellow-beings, seva towards one's fellow-beings and a firm unshakeable intellectual conviction of this jnana, coupled with a daily reflection on one's own reactions to the world. A complete integration of one's intellect, feelings and actions is required to practice SAW in life.
I believe that all the sattvic behavior - sattvic traits mentioned in the Gita - detachment, loving kindness, sympathy for others, a desire to work for the welfare of others, a desire to work for the welfare of others, serenity, etc. All these would come in automatically. A lack of concern for self-aggrandizement - material or otherwise... these are the behaviors which would reflect a growth in spirituality. Swami Ranganathananda-ji (a former President of Ramakrishna Mission) was once asked how one knows that one is growing spiritually and he answered that growth of peace inwardly and a desire to serve others outwardly are its twin expressions.

When asked for illustrations of SAW in their own organizations, the responses indicated an application of the *being* aspect in behaviors with an emphasis on the attitude behind the action. One such instance was related as follows:

It happened during my initial years in the Ramakrishna Mission when I had gone to our Kankhal ashrama - which is now a big hospital - and I went to the OPD where a number of wounded people were regularly dressed. Many of the wounds were such that I could not even look at them without a shudder passing down my spine. And an elderly swamiji was dressing a wound. I cannot tell you about the expression on the monk's face as he was dressing that abominable wound. He was totally serene, calm and composed as if he was offering prayers in the worship-room even as he dressed the wound. As if, he was operating from the highest possible plane while doing the work. Remembering that particular incident still makes my hair stand on end. Then I was told that the monk has taken over patients for whom the doctors had ordered amputation of limbs. Through his loving kindness and attention to wound-dressing, he has had those limbs come alive once again. And, this has happened not with one, not with two but countless patients. People now form queues to be dressed by this particular monk. He is not a doctor, he is not even a trained compounder but still patients come in queues to be administered by him. He used to dress even the private parts of women and the women too would not feel that he was a man who was dressing it.
That incident taught me what was meant by spirituality at work. Earlier I used to mistake it for prayers in the worship-room and other such practices but that day I learnt that it is the attitude with which you take up any work that you do. Are you approaching your work with the highest state that you can conceive of? You don't just throw the flowers at the feet of the image you are worshipping... you offer it with full care and out of a fullness of heart... that is the spirit with which one has to approach every action in one's workplace too. What is the state of your

mind while you are doing your work? That would determine the extent to which you have been able to spiritualize your work. Is it different from the state that your mind gets into when you are offering your prayers or carrying out your spiritual practices? In case they are different then it is only mundane work... you have not been able to imbibe aspect of spirituality in your work.

It really does not matter what sort of work you do. You could be administering a college, teaching students, or even cutting vegetables for cooking... none of that matter! Every action can be spiritualized. It is only a question of cultivating the right attitude towards it. Have you heard of Brother Lawrence? His only task was to cut vegetables and he wrote in his book 'Practice of the Presence of God' that even as he cut vegetables he would get the same feeling as if he were in communion with Christ.

I did not get that feeling initially but when I saw that monk for a few minutes, I got the feeling as if I was sitting in a temple and the priest in front of me was making offerings to the Divine. That was the sense that I got. My mind was uplifted to a very high level.

I think that *that* is spirituality at work.

One can identify in the illustration above the being of individual spirituality reflected in the doing. For the other non-profits however, the manifestation of SAW inhered in the social benefit work that the organization was engaged in (what can be termed *doing*). A typical response from an interview in those organizations was that the organization was not into profit-making and its activities too were for social benefit and that itself indicated how spirituality was being expressed in action. While this theme was rather characteristic of those non-profits that were not explicitly-spiritual, even the explicitly-spiritual category respondents considered it a significant indicator of expansion of one's identity. It can be seen that this position is consistent with the SAW theme of larger than oneself.

Further, a majority of this study's respondents suggested that SAW would manifest in the form of the practitioner's personal qualities. Adherence to values one believes in, being unselfish in one's thoughts and actions, and integrity and authenticity in one's actions [as reflected in the dictum 'to thine own self be true'] emerged prominently as illustrations of SAW's manifestation at the individual level.

Another SAW manifestation theme, characteristic of explicitly-spiritual organizations' respondents, was that of staying in the witnessing mode: *sakshi bhava*. Closely related to the other theme of detached action and unselfishness, *sakshi bhava* refers to an attitude of consciously avoiding habitual and instinctual reactions to stimuli, based as these reactions usually are in egocentric notions about the world and ourselves. This specific attitude of being an unconcerned observer allows bypassing or witnessing disturbances arising out of the external stimuli or those emerging from the conscious and sub-conscious mind. It has been routinely asserted that thoughts that are generally very difficult to negotiate can be gradually overcome by adopting the approach of *sakshi bhava*.

Another theme that emerged prominently was role-based. A sizeable section of the respondents referred to SAW being manifested not only in dutiful observance of what one is supposed to do in a specific role but in making it the best that one is capable of. The attitude of 'doing one's best' thus emerged as a specific manifestation of SAW. In the words of a respondent belonging to an explicitly-spiritual organization, this aspect related to the pursuit of perfection in life: "your work should be as perfect as the perfection that's within you." The issue of integrity and wholeness while being a part of SAW's conceptualization was also seen as a way to practice SAW. As a respondent mentioned, "Expressing oneself... being one with the work that one is doing... The question to ask is 'Am I able to express who I am through this work?' My work is not separate from who I am."

Issues relating to the traditional Indian ideas and the concept of karma-yoga referred by many respondents in relation with the practice of spirituality at work shall be explored in detail in the discussion and conclusions chapter later.

At the organizational level, adherence to a code of ethics and not harming one's environment emerged as major features of SAW manifestation. Ability to ward off temptations and stay true to one's mission was a theme that was reflected in many incidents. One such instance was related as:

> In 1996 or 1997, we got an offer for training teachers for 50 weeks per year. However, according to the arrangement that was being offered, we would not have had the privilege of selecting whom we wanted to impart training to. We were in a rather tight financial position at that point of time and needed the money badly. However, our founder brought that issue before us all and shared the offer with us. All of us said that we could ill-afford taking up a project that has no link with our ideology and philosophy of social transformation through education. It would have reduced us to being a mere service-provider, which is not what we wanted to be. We declined the offer in spite of its munificent nature. I would feel that it demonstrates a rather strong sense of spirituality and fidelity to purpose.

For the explicitly-spiritual organizations, SAW manifested at the organizational level in a routine that featured time for spiritual activities, opportunities to relate all decisions to their impact on the spiritual character of the organization. One respondent placed it in the following fashion:

> The organization should provide an environment that makes experimentation with the inner life possible. However, a discipline does need to be maintained: a code of ethics and morality would serve as the smrti for organizational members. This is a principle that would not distinguish between a spiritual and a non-spiritual organization, for in reality there is nothing non-spiritual. No extra-cosmic entities need to be invoked for this purpose. [06:40] Swami Vivekananda said that if a fisherman believed in vedanta he would be a better fisherman: he need not invoke "spirituality" for that purpose...
> I believe that this is after all what the monastic and other spiritual organizations have been designed to do. These organizations have been designed to help those with the calling and those with the aspiration of being spiritual people, being devotees of a deity... it is to provide them with an environment where they can practice and they can grow more than what they would have been able to do outside. Now the question is what are the organizational features of such organizations that help them help those who choose to come in. I suppose that those common features would be:
> 1. Very stringent rules and discipline that include the basic norms of morality, which gives great environment of spiritual practice
> 2. A focus on encouraging brotherhood that helps to create a spiritual community
> 3. A sense of mission relating the spiritual organization to contribute through social welfare.
> Taking care of these would help the organization encourage:
> i. personal development meaning spiritual development for its members;
> ii. a sense of well-knit spiritual community; and
> iii. its members to go out and relate to the society in a manner of meaningful service.

A specific feature of manifesting SAW was observed in one explicitly-non-spiritual non-profit that was redefining its Vision and Mission statement. During the time of data collection many respondents seemed particularly energized and enthusiastic. The common reason for many was their participation in the Vision and mission statement re-definition process. Since the non-profit had already been in the field for more than 30 years the needs that had earlier driven it were no longer so urgent. It was felt by the top management team that though the recently inducted professionals may have been able to word those documents better, getting the buy-in from the older workers was equally critical. Hence, the process was initiated from the lowest level of the hierarchy and it built a tremendous sense of belonging within the organization.

To recapitulate, the respondents of this study expressed their opinions on both the personal expression of spirituality and its organizational manifestation. The personal expression focused more on the attitude that one develops till it becomes a part of oneself. This attitude would then sacralize the mundane and permeate each and every activity that one undertakes. From the organizational manifestation perspective, a major part would be in terms of the less selfish activities that the organization takes up and also the opportunity structures that are consciously created to help individuals in their spiritual quest. The employee perception of opportunity structures inside the organization could be aided by provision of certain facilities such as prayer and meditation rooms, inviting explicitly spiritual individuals for discourses and talks and institutionalizing processes that respect each individual and provide for a certain code of ethics.

5.3.4 Importance of the context for SAW
This study argued that appropriate organizational conditions may perhaps be necessary for the practice of SAW. It was to test this argument that organizations belonging to two different categories – explicitly-spiritual and otherwise - had been selected for the study. It was thus of interest to examine the role organizational conditions could play in facilitating or hindering the practice of SAW. The respondents were asked to relate their experiences with respect to the opportunity structure present in their organizations for practicing SAW.
The respondents largely agreed that the organizational opportunity structure for SAW practice may perhaps be critical. Amongst those from explicitly-spiritual organizations the option of leaving the organization did not arise at all as their SAW expression needs – an issue central to their individual lives - were pretty much satisfied in the current organization. Opportunities available in the present organization for such discussions and individual spiritual practices were cited as the major advantage of staying on and not seeking other alternatives.

Amongst the not-explicitly spiritual organizations community gatherings, common prayer sessions invoking social benefit, visits of the religious and spiritual leaders to engage in "spiritual discussions" emerged as major facilitating conditions. "We get lost in the daily work-load and emergencies otherwise," was the common refrain. However, it needs to be mentioned that such activities can not be seen in isolation from the overall culture of the organization. This fact was brought to light with a particular incident when the organization invited a certain spiritual individual for conducting a session on stress relief. That the top management team chose to stay away from the function was not appreciated by the employees who did attend the session. "Is it that only the ones lower down in the hierarchy *need* these sessions and the higher-ups are immune to these pressures? But one does not see evidence of this in their encounters with us… instead it would appear that they need to de-stress more than we do." It can be inferred from the instance above that SAW initiatives can not be applied in a piece meal fashion but would need an appropriate organizational culture to take root.

Further, another intriguing question suggested by Gurkiewicz & Giacalone (2004) was about the experience of the less-spiritual individuals in more-spiritual organizations and vice versa. In response to the specific issue of a non-spiritual person in a more-spiritual organization and vice-versa raised by Jurkiewicz and Giacalone (2004), the results from this study were rather ambiguous as can be inferred from the MANOVA results that were presented earlier in section 5.2.1. The issue of person-organization fit reflected in the ambiguous findings indeed may need a great deal of further research as suggested by Jurkiewicz and Giacalone themselves.

5.3.5 The contested SAW consequences

Previous research has seen intense debates on the issue of consequences that can be expected from SAW. While the theologically-inclined scholars do not take kindly to the organizational performance implications from utilizing SAW, those in management research disciplines fail to appreciate how a concept that does not lend itself to improving firm performance shall ever be adopted in present-day organizations.

From the interview responses, both the positions were supported. While even amongst the explicitly-spiritual organizations, a few interviewees indicated instrumental outcomes from spirituality the majority appeared to support the following position:

> I feel that the major consequence [of SAW] would be more spirituality. Transformation of the persons involved their own obviously but the others - their colleagues, seniors, juniors as well as those who come in contact with them in their daily course of work - all of them will also not fail to be touched by the very glow that comes from within through the practice of spirituality at work.
> I also believe that the quality and quantity of work will also improve.
> Further, there are many problems particularly conflicts will significantly reduce, both in scale and intensity.

> Moreover, in the long run I think, the nature of work itself may change if spirituality is sufficiently practiced. A profit oriented organization may not remain all that profit-oriented. In fact, it is very unlikely that it will remain solely profit-oriented. It may still make profits but that will become secondary.

The emphasis in the above excerpt is on the transformational potential of spirituality practice, not only for the individuals concerned but also for collectivities like organizations. However, not all interviewees viewed spirituality as an end in itself and instead quoted the usual arguments in SAW research about spirituality leading to more satisfied, committed and happier individuals in organizations who would produce and serve more to raise profits. On being asked about the potential consequences of SAW, such individuals answered in the following words: "you would have a more transparent and disciplined workforce and a more energetic environment at work featured by Health, Well-Being and Longevity" and "For Individuals: authenticity, punctuality, devotion and lack of hypocrisy i.e., cultivation of integrity; and at the organizational level: mutual respect and a more open and relaxed environment".

A few respondents expressed apprehensions about the SAW practice being taken advantage of by others: "If one's sense of spirituality is manifested externally one may be made fun of, in today's secularized society." A similar sentiment was expressed by another interviewee, "you may become too good for the 'bad people' and could then be taken for granted." However, it must be added that such ambivalent feelings about SAW consequences were not very common amongst this study's respondents.

In the next chapter, explanations for the findings in this chapter will be elaborated upon and implications for further theorization and practice shall be explored. The results will also be compared with existing literature to examine the contributions from this study and discuss its limitations.

Chapter 6: Discussion and Conclusions

This chapter presents a review of the study and discusses its findings. Drawing from the findings, it draws implications for the theorization and practice of spirituality at work and lists the key limitations of this research. Recommendations for future studies conclude the chapter.

6.1 Review of the study

Spirituality at work has recently emerged as an appealing trend in organizations. The more commonly cited reasons for this interest include a fast changing employment contract inside organizations, one that no longer rewards loyalty with employment security. Further, the changing socio-cultural conditions are also argued to have led individuals to examine issues of meaningfulness and purposefulness inside organizations. Scholars also claim that wary of being forced to perform in an atomistic fashion, employees today are more open to exploring community-based relationships beyond selfish interests in the workplace.

Beyond the antecedents for the rise of interest in SAW, conceptual ambiguity remains the norm in SAW research. From reiki and feng-shui to using yoga and meditation inside organizations to an individual search for meaning and purpose, SAW has been related to all these and many other practices inside the workplace. A conceptual convergence has however been detected in the academic writings in the area (Sheep, 2004) and consequently this study selected three themes as representing the central features of SAW: integrity and wholeness, meaningful work, and larger than oneself. An attempt was made to validate these three SAW themes in this study and look into other themes that may be relevant to understanding SAW.

Most of the scholarly literature on SAW has so far focused on SAW conceptualization and its potential benefits to individuals and organizations. Relatively fewer studies have looked at the ways in which spirituality can be manifested in an organizational context. Similarly, aligned with the traditional individual-focus, organizational context's influence on SAW practice too has been neglected. This study tried to examine both the issues: while on one hand it examined the signs of SAW's expression inside organizations on the other hand it tried to compare the experiences of organizational members in two distinct organizational types. It was hoped that a comparison of lived experiences in explicitly-spiritual organizations and the other nonprofits would throw up interesting data on the influence of the organizational context for the practice of SAW.

Earlier literature on SAW has convincingly argued in favor of the relevance of spirituality for organizations and has even linked it to the many benefits that would accrue to organizations

(Giacalone & Jurkiewicz, 2003a). Reave (2005) has earlier linked the various characteristics of leadership effectiveness with the practice of spiritual ideals and values. However, not much evidence has yet been presented on how those benefits are realized by individuals and organizations.

To explore these issues, it was decided to use a hybrid quantitative-and-qualitative design to examine the antecedents, conceptualization, manifestation, organizational influence and consequences of spirituality at work.

6.2 Overall profile of respondents

The survey sample consisted of 169 respondents from six nonprofit organizations – three belonging to explicitly-spiritual category and three others. 114 among them also agreed for one-on-one interviews.

While a broad outline of the demographic distribution of the respondents has been provided in the earlier chapters, it is useful to elaborate on its salient features in this chapter.

To explore issues relating to SAW expression at all levels of the organizations special care was exercised to include respondents across the hierarchy in each organization. In four organizations, the founders and current executive heads of the organization made time to take part in the study.

In terms of tenure, the respondents ranged from those who had just joined the organization to those who had been with the organization since its birth or had been in the organization for more than 20 years. Almost 30% of respondents had spent between 10 and 20 years in their organization, 20% between 5 and 10 years, and the rest were equally divided in the three categories of less than 2 years, 2 to 5 years and more than 20 years. Four organizations had the largest number of employees who had been with the organization for between 10 and 20 years and only one organization had most of its respondents in the younger category (within five years). Interestingly, the demographic variables did not have an impact on the outcome variables. The reason could be the well-documented effect of strong cultures that make specific demands from all its members.

In terms of educational qualifications, the sample was well-spread out with 40% of respondents being postgraduates, 31% had a graduation degree, and over 15% held a doctorate degree and the rest were evenly divided between a professional degree and 10th standard education. However, in two departures from this general trend, this distribution was skewed towards lesser education for organization 4 and higher education for organization 6.

6.3 The antecedents of SAW

Previous SAW literature argues that the business environment has changed dramatically in recent years and it is this change in socio-economic conditions that prompts individuals to look for meaning and purpose in their workplaces. Decline in traditional opportunities for community (Duchon & Plowman, 2005), developments in technology that allows people to enjoy more leisure time (Neck & Milliman, 1994), an increasing exposure to alternative, more contemplative lifestyles (Neal, Lichtenstein, & Banner, 1999), and a society moving higher on Maslow's hierarchy of needs (Len Tischler, 1999) have been placed forward as the specific factors that are guiding the SAW movement today. This study tried to validate these assertions and seek confirmation from empirical evidence if the socio-economic environment indeed was sensed to have changed radically to have people engage in such pursuits.

A related issue in literature is a contradictory assessment of who drives the movement. The employee-pull variant of this argument links the current upsurge of interest in SAW with employee readiness to engage with such concerns while the organization-push relates it to the organizations seeing in SAW a possibility of improving job satisfaction and organizational commitment among its employees. From the data that was gathered in this study it appeared that except for the explicitly spiritual organizations that actively promoted and supported the pursuit of SAW within the organization the other nonprofits largely left it to the individual concerned to engage with SAW.

Further, as reported in section 5.4.1, it was obvious from the interview responses that while a few respondents were indeed concerned about a society that is becoming increasingly materialistic, most did not link their desire to engage in SAW to the socio-economic conditions. Instead, a majority credited their inclination to spirituality and its practice to early influence from their families and later contacts with inspiring individuals and spiritual organizations. Further, the community feeling that was cultivated in sample organizations prompted individuals to look for a beyond-oneself identity. Spiritually disengaging experiences in earlier organizations too emerged as the motivation for a few respondents to seek involvement in a workplace that was more 'spirit-friendly'. In this respect the findings from this study to some extent corroborate the position in literature that current organizational climates may well have become toxic for sustaining superior performance (Frost, 2003; Kriger & Seng, 2005; Pfeffer, 1998) and may force their employees to search for more spiritually conducive organizations (Neal, 2000).

However, it needs to be added that the sample organizations were rather monochromatic and a similar study from the corporate sector may be required to confirm the findings from the for-profit business context.

At the organizational level, the wish of the top management team to have the employees take up SAW as a way to find more meaning and involvement in their daily chores was linked to their own convictions emerging from early family influence and contact with spiritually inclined individuals and organizations. What did not find support in this study was the position that the organizations were looking at SAW as a conscious way to increase job satisfaction and promote organizational commitment, as argued in a section of SAW literature (Forray & Stork, 2002). While a few top management team members in one organization did feel that the mechanical way in which their employees engage with their work could be improved with incorporation of a more spiritual outlook, the inherent sensitive nature of the issue (the reason for many respondents preferring to underplay their spirituality in Mitroff & Denton, 1999b) held them from openly espousing and promoting this position. The top management team did try to promote the practice of SAW subtly by inviting speakers who could be identified as being spiritual to deliver lectures on "the right way" to engage with one's work. The experiment however did not work as well owing to suspicions about the motives behind organizing such lectures. The employees also felt that the top management team was adopting a 'holier than thou' attitude by not participating in the event itself, implying thereby that it was only the lower level employees who needed such inputs. The findings of this study thus do not support the frequently asserted position in literature that interest in SAW results from the discontinuous socio-economic and cultural change brought about due to changed environment.

Instead, the findings place emphasis on the early experiences of individuals in families and community which determine the individual values.

However, the study does support the position that individuals may be looking for organizations that are more "spirit-friendly" and make available opportunity structures that enable individuals to express their spirituality at work.

6.4 Understanding of SAW

A hotly debated issue in SAW research has been that of concept definition. Two strands of this debate were explored in the present study: religion-spirituality distinction and components of SAW.

Most of prevalent SAW definitions center on distinguishing spirituality from religion owing to "dangers of proselytizing and invasion of privacy" (Reave, 2005:656). This apprehension has led to a position that identifies and defines spirituality in *nonreligion* terms (Harvey, 2001). The controversial relationship between religion and spirituality was raised and elaborated on by many respondents of this study. A significant majority of respondents argued that spirituality was inextricably intertwined with religion. Even though it may be argued that these results can only be expected from the explicitly spiritual organizations owing to their perceived predisposition in favor of religion, more than half the respondents from the other nonprofits too held the same opinion. As for the other respondents, only a few (4 out of 114 interviewees) felt that linking the issues of religion and spirituality might harm the secular organizational ethos.

This finding is in stark contrast to that reported from the western countries. Mitroff and Denton (1999), for instance, reported that 60% of their respondents had a positive view of spirituality and a negative one of religion and another 8% had a negative view of both religion and spirituality. Thus, while over two-thirds of Mitroff and Denton's respondents carried a negative impression of religion, hardly 3.5% of this study's respondents supported that position. While in part, the finding could be attributed to 50% of the present study's sample being from explicitly spiritual organizations that can be said to harbor a more charitable view of religion, this proportion was considerably high among the respondents from the other nonprofits. The primary reason for the finding could be a sample that may be more biased in favor of seeing religion in a positive light. A comparable study from the for-profit business sector may help test if a similar view of religion and spirituality is upheld by the general population too.

Further, while references to studies that examine the cultural context of Indian managers shall also be made in subsequent sections, culture-specific reasons that could explain this divergence of perception regarding religion and spirituality are provided below.

One of the probable reasons for this finding that counters most of existing SAW research is that religion may be construed as a way of life in India rather than as a set of commandments emerging from scriptures (Sinha & Kanungo, 1997). Further, in contrast to the western experience with struggles for church-state separation (for an alternative viewpoint, see Speck, 2005) that leads to a suspicious view of religion in public life (Dean, 2004), Hinduism offers a "potentially hospitable attitude" (Sharma, 2005) towards a secular state. It can be argued that a similar generous attitude - drawing from this essential feature of India's dominant religion - may perhaps also exist towards retention of secular organizational ethos. Further, the position in existing SAW research that argues for separation of religion and spirituality in the workplace based on the potentially divisive role that religion could play too is countered by the conventional nonsectarian nature of modern Hinduism (Sharma, 2005). The position is further substantiated by the emergence of tolerance as modern Hinduism's distinctive feature (Hefner, 1998; Sinha, 1997). Sharma (2005) argues that while religious tolerance has always been a hallmark of Hinduism, the religion's modern interpretation places an emphatic accent on this particular feature.

The findings of this research thus corroborate the position that religion and spirituality are not necessarily differentiated in eastern cultures (Shahjahan, 2005) and provide proof from the context of Indian nonprofits.

It needs to be added, however, that in the current scenario the role of religion in fomenting fundamentalist tendencies has come to the fore. While religion may well serve as a cementing factor for the believers in a particular faith, its role in confirming stereotypes about the other to incite social unrest would merit a broader examination of the context. Having discussed the place of religion in SAW on the basis of research findings, the next issue in understanding SAW was the absence of a widely accepted definition of SAW. Such a definition not being available, scholars have tried to include such diverse aspects that render a precise operationalization impractical. While there are scholars who argue that a single definition is impossible for a construct as subjective as SAW (Gull & Doh, 2004) others argue that the concept is not so elusive as it is "confused and imprecise" (Brown, 2003). A conceptual convergence, however, has been suggested as emerging in SAW literature (Sheep, 2004) which was further fine-tuned in this study – see section 2.3.2 - to point to three themes: integrity and wholeness, meaningful work, and larger than oneself. These three themes were supported in this study. While all three themes found resonance with the respondents from explicitly spiritual organizations, the two specific themes that appealed in particular for those in other nonprofits were: meaningful work and larger than oneself. The reason for such an emphasis may be related to being engaged with activities that go beyond just earning a living, and the desire to serve the larger community that motivated these individuals to join the nonprofits.

Moreover, a divergence was apparent in the responses referring to the theme of larger than oneself: for respondents from the explicitly spiritual organizations it embraced the transcendental notions of association with the Divine, whereas its sense for those in the other nonprofits was restricted to one's work community and the society that one serves. It can thus be inferred that the context too may have an influence in determining the understanding of SAW that individuals employ. Where the context favors a sense of wholeness that incorporates aspiration for the Divine, individuals include that meaning in their understanding of SAW. Alternatively, where the situation focuses on meaningful contribution towards the society, individuals' attitudes towards understanding spirituality at work reflects the same emphasis.

Beyond the three SAW themes that had been culled from current research literature, several other issues emerged from interview data. The necessity of a spiritual practice to sustain one's aspiration was found to be another imperative for understanding SAW. Respondents related this idea to the small rituals that they engaged in at work or the other practices that fed and fuelled the aspiration for the spiritual.

Clark (2002) had earlier argued that in spiritual matters an intellectual appreciation of fundamental beliefs alone may not lead to experience and that various practices may help access the spiritual response. This component of spiritual practices could thus be related to the lived nature of spirituality at work to bridge the gap between a theoretical conceptualization and its practice.

Another feature that needs to be emphasized is that despite the focus on the workplace in the present study, respondents found it difficult to restrict the sense of spirituality to the workplace alone. A related study had earlier found that managers in rapidly changing environments integrate their spirituality with their work rather than separate their private life from their public life (Delbecq, 1999). In relating it to the fundamental nature of spirituality, Emmons (1999; 2005) had argued that the Sacred was the very "core of life" and thus can not be restricted to only one arena of one's life.

The present study's interviewees agreed with the position that spirituality inheres not only in certain practices but also in its influence over all aspects of one's life. It can thus be concluded that the three components of Spirituality at work that had been taken as starting points for this study cannot be restricted to the workplace alone but would affect one's entire life.

Further, for many in the explicitly spiritual organizations the attitude of *samataa* (roughly translated as same-sightedness or equanimity) and *niraapeksha bhaava* (action without hankering for its fruits) was synonymous with SAW. However, as these issues relate to the practice of SAW they shall be taken up in the next section.

From the foregoing it may thus be concluded that the findings of the present study countered the prevalent notion of separating religion from spirituality in SAW. The findings also supported the three-way conceptualization of SAW – integrity and wholeness; meaningful work; and larger than oneself – and added the issue of spiritual practice as another component of SAW. The findings also suggest that while the focus may be on spirituality at work, the influence of spiritual concerns would be reflected in all spheres of one's life.

Another related issue that can be adduced from the discussion above is the crucial importance of the context. Many of the above findings could be related to the sample itself which would have reflected in the position on religion and spirituality. At another level, the understandings and definition of SAW that is adopted would depend on the organizational environment. While the broad SAW categories could be accepted in general, their precise formulation shall have to be modified on the basis of the prevalent context.

6.5 Manifestation and expression of SAW

Yet another significant issue this study looked at was the assertion that organizations – being seen as institutionalized environments - are fundamentally incompatible with spiritual strivings (Ashforth & Pratt, 2003). Since the argument assumes that spirituality is essentially an individual phenomenon, it was of interest to examine if expression of spirituality could go beyond the individual level. The previous chapter has shown that the interviewees in this study had divergent ideas about manifesting SAW at individual and organizational levels.

At the individual level of expression, the person could focus on *Being* and *Doing* aspects of SAW expression. The *Being* aspect of SAW expression focused on who the person was while the *Doing* focused on what the person does.

The *Being* aspects of individual SAW focused on the beliefs and values referring to what the individual should be feeling and acting on. The eastern concepts of *samataa* (same-sighted-ness), *niraapeeksha bhaava* (not hankering after the effects of actions), and *saakshi bhaava* (assuming the attitude of a witness so as to remain unattached to one's actions) were commonly placed forward as the fitting attitudes for practicing SAW.

In the *Doing* category of SAW expression, emphasis shifted to behaviors and actions one could be engaged in to reflect adherence to SAW principles. The most common such behaviors and actions were either role-based where the emphasis was placed on doing one's best or relational where harmonious interactions with one's colleagues were stressed. Essentially, these two features apply to the practice of individual values while working. Many respondents – and not necessarily only those from explicitly spiritual organizations – alluded to the traditional attitude of karma yoga for the practice of SAW. This was one idea that appeared often across both organizational types. The following two quotations explain the theme:

> Spirituality at work should mean the work you do today is better than what you had done yesterday. And the work that you are doing is uplifting your character and revealing more of the Divine within you. It is not something that has to be done at the cost of work or excellence in work. Far from it!

> [when asked for a specific incident illustrating SAW practice] I remember an old monk who was putting up in Deoghar ashrama and trying to pin a few sheets of paper together. He took great care to see that the sharp end of the pin did not protrude and was hidden between the sheets. He explained to me that it ensured that no one got hurt while handling the papers. That showed the sensitivity, the subtle approach that one takes to every action in one's life. I remember being told by monks about karma-yoga and though most of it went above my head then there is this one incident I still remember. I remember this elderly monk whom I was serving once and in broad daylight he asked me to switch on the light. I complied and switched on the light. Immediately he said, "Why that noise: so much of sound should not come." I switched it off and on again without as much of sound and then he said something very wonderful about karma-yoga: "I have planted the seed. If the earth is ready for it, it will sprout."

As it refers to the traditional Indian concept of yoga and the attendant aim of life, a summary of the associated positions is considered useful. One of the masters who reinterpreted

Hindu traditions to appeal to the rational sensibilities of the age was Swami Vivekananda. In his words, "EACH soul is potentially Divine. The goal is to manifest this Divinity within by controlling nature, external and internal. Do this either by work or worship or psychic control or philosophy - by one or more all of these - and be free. This is whole of RELIGION." Interestingly, one of the four major paths that Swami Vivekananda recommends for reaching the goal of religion is that of work. Referred to as karma yoga, Swami Vivekananda explicated on the concept:

> What is Karma-Yoga? The knowledge of the secret of work. We see the whole universe is working. For what? For salvation, for liberty, from the atom to the highest being, working for the one end, liberty of the mind, for the body, for the spirit. All things are always trying to get freedom, flying away from bondage... we learn from karma-yoga the secret of work, the method of work, the organizing power of work... Karma-Yoga makes a science of work... Work is inevitable, it must be so, but we should work to the highest purpose.

Unattached action is the basis of karma yoga and implies a complete focus on the task while excluding all diversionary thoughts about the benefits that may accrue to oneself by its successful accomplishment. The ideal of karma yoga forcefully rejects the view that spirituality and materiality are necessarily opposed to each other. Instead, the doctrine advises the use of the material until a time comes when one may transcend it. In honoring the self-transformation potential of each individual it suggests that the material objects and relationships be used to progressively overcome one's attachment towards them.

Emmons (1999) in investigating the place of religion and spirituality in the psychology of personality related the issues of personality growth with self-transformation. Relating the transformation of personality "at its very centre" with sanctification, Emmons claimed that even as the spiritual striving provides the individual with the ways and means to pursue one's life, "sanctification carries the process one step further in moving from individual goals and concerns to a patterned organization within the person over time directing the person toward spiritual perfection" (ibid.:880). The spiritual life is thus seen as "a lifelong process of growth towards holiness and progress towards the ultimate goal of perfection" (ibid.:881).

In the Indian tradition, another associated idea that explains the focus on unselfish work mentioned by many of the interviewees is that each thought and action is assumed to leave a *samskara* (an impression) in one's mind. These *samskaras* then drive the person onward to habitual tendencies and actions. It is conceived that a detached ego will not gather impressions and the individual would thus move towards the *summum bonum* of life: freedom or liberation.

At this point it would be useful to point out that issues relating to the themes of self-transcendence are not restricted to the religious organizations or the nonprofit sector but are being increasingly cited in general management and academic literature as well as business management classrooms. In his book *Good to Great*, Collins (2001) identified a few companies that report incredible turnaround performance and attributed their phenomenal success to Level 5 leadership. In the progression from Level 1 to Level 5 leadership, the ego of Level 4 leaders gets in the way of effective performance. However, the level 5 leaders are marked by extreme personal humility and thus can take away the spotlight from themselves to focus on the collective good. Relating the concept to a business management classroom, Pielstick (2005) reports encouraging findings when issues relating to transcending one's ego and integrating spiritual issues with business leadership are investigated. Issues relating to ego-transcendence in relation to leadership effectiveness are dealt with in greater detail in Parameshwar (2005).

At the organizational level of SAW expression, reference was frequently made to the activities being undertaken by the organization, the disciplinary routines being followed and rituals that were a part of organizational processes. For many respondents SAW was manifested organizationally when the organization or its members did not gain materially from its activities. However, a few interviewees disagreed that selfless activities undertaken by the organization manifested organizational SAW. For them organizational spirituality was expressed in the nature of explanations provided for every action or decision: if the explanations belonged to an overarching framework of spiritual principles, then and then alone was SAW manifested at the organizational level. A closer scrutiny reveals that the response is characteristic of the Directing organization as defined by Ashforth and Pratt (2003) - see section 2.3.6 for further details - where the individual spiritual strivings were driven by the organization. Not surprisingly again, such responses were received from the explicitly spiritual organizations that are characterized by strong cultures.

With the activities and behaviors that displayed the practice of SAW at organizational level there were also some pointers about what would not be compatible with an organizational SAW orientation:

> Maybe an explicit task orientation... an overemphasis on the outer environment that focuses on the instrumental results of the tasks carried out and to a certain extent all organizational politics, if I may use the word, [dysfunctional politics, would it be?]... Yes, it does not matter much for a spiritual organization to not be led democratically, for it not to have a retirement age, if it is mired in poverty... in fact, it might be better in a sense for it to remain poor...

That the same aberration was not apparent in the respondent's organization was asserted when the following incidents were forwarded as illustrations of SAW practice:

> There was this brahmachari who was given the charge of putting up the gobar gas plant in Deoghar ashrama. The whole project failed and the money spent literally went down the drain. When the brahmachari reported this to the secretary maharaj Swami Suhitananda-ji and regretted the loss of money, Suhitananda-ji immediately snapped back, "Why do you say that? It is not the money that is important... it is the experience that you have gained through it that is important." Even in general I have seen the scolding that one gets from senior monks is never about the work that one has or should have done but always about issues related to the values in work.
> There is this other incident that I remember now. I have seen that it is easy to lose yourself in the deluge of work when you enter a new work-site. I was a newcomer into the organization and I was teaching students... the time when meditation becomes grim after the initial romance and work proves to be easier. So, after the prayers when it was time to sit for

> meditation I softly walked into the library and switched on the lights. I was going through the books there, taking them off the shelf when a monk... a senior monk... came and scolded me harshly and asked me what I was doing. I told him that I was preparing for the class. He commanded me to switch off the lights and go off to the temple immediately and he stayed there, glowering at me till I complied, mumbling excuses all the while. But that again displayed the focus of organizational spirituality where it cares more about your spiritual practice rather than your work.

It can be concluded from the foregoing discussion on the manifestation of SAW that organizations need not necessarily constrain the expression of spiritual concerns and may indeed provide facilitating conditions for its practice. Spirituality may be expressed in the workplace at individual and organizational levels. At the individual level, the focus on self-transformation through the work one is engaged in and progressive movement towards perfection could be taken as the expression of SAW. However, at the organizational level, beyond the unselfish nature of activities undertaken by the organization, spirituality would be reflected in the rationale provided for each action taken or decision made.

6.6 Does the P-O fit matter for SAW?

It was argued in the study that apart from the individual-pull factor or the organization-push factors that have been routinely cited as the determinants of SAW practice and its outcomes, the P-O fit may perhaps explain the behaviors and outcomes better. To that end, individual SAW needs and organizational SAW supplies were examined in this study and the scores related to various outcome variables.

It was found – see section 5.2.3 for details - the associations with outcomes variables grew progressively stronger in this sequence: individual SAW needs, P-O fit on SAW, and organizational SAW supplies. Thus while the proposition that P-O fit would be more strongly associated with outcome variables against the individual needs and organizational SAW supplies was not supported, the results nevertheless suggest that the current preoccupation with SAW at individual level may need to be reworked to take into account the influence of the context. The results from this study thus suggest that more efforts are needed at the organizational level so the workplace is seen as an enabling environment for meeting individual SAW needs.

This finding assumes importance since Mitroff and Denton (1999) reported on the prevalence of "you go first" game inside organizations. While the employees in Mitroff and Denton's study expected their supervisors to make the first move in raising spiritual issues, the supervisors argued that they themselves would have no objections if their employees did so. The game resulted in the spiritual issues not being raised at all. To this extent, this study provides the first ever evidence of the relevance of the interactive effects of individual and workplace spirituality pointed out as a promising area in SAW research (Jurkiewicz & Giacalone, 2004).

The relatively less importance of individual SAW needs and the greater importance of organizational SAW supplies in the Indian context can be related to the concepts of "contextual sensitivity" and "balancing" advocated by Sinha & Kanungo (1997). Sinha and Kanungo argue that easterners, owing to their cultural heritage, are more likely to behave in a context-dependent fashion than do their western counterparts. It is claimed that the context-independent rule-governed environment perspective that can be applied in western societies does not hold for India. Instead, the Indian changes oneself to do justice to the demands placed by the environment (Ibid.:95). The influence of context sensitivity may well be the cause of the greater role of organizational culture in Indian organizations than it does elsewhere (Sinha, 1997).

Drawing from the above, the finding that individual SAW needs exert lesser influence on work outcomes as compared to the organizational SAW supplies is probably not surprising. A related issue that emerges from the present finding is a re-examination of the SAW prescriptions in literature. *Scholars may need to consider the impact of the cultural context…* Wider studies examining a variety of cultural contexts are therefore required to test the generalize-ability of various SAW recommendations found in literature and examine the various other contingency factors that may operate.

6.7 The importance of organizational context in SAW

The extant literature presents SAW as a panacea that would work regardless of its context. In contrast, this study argued that different organizations may perhaps feature varying opportunity structures for the practice of SAW and sought out to test it in two dissimilar organizational environments.

The findings affirmed that the opportunity structures could vary even within the nonprofit sector. However, it needs to be added that while constructing the homogeneous sets of organizations in quantitative analysis, the six organizations were not divided in neat explicitly spiritual and other nonprofits categories even though the organizational clusters formed did display homogeneity in terms of opportunity structures. From this observation, it can be inferred that the organizations may perhaps lie on a continuum of spiritual opportunity structures. While on one end of this continuum would lie organizations for whom spirituality is their *raison d'etre*, on the other could be placed organizations that are not concerned at all about spiritual issues.

Nonetheless, analysis suggested that the explicitly spiritual organizations were found to provide better opportunities for accessing spiritual resources – both internal and organizational – owing to the organizational focus on fostering spirituality. The organizational focus was reflected in the primary emphasis being given to spiritual objectives ahead of the organizational performance features as indicated by the many 'spiritual practice *versus* performance focus' experiences that have been related in the earlier sections. The difference in organizational focus was also accompanied by statistically significant differences in the individual SAW needs scores across the two categories of organizations. The result thus suggests that individuals too select organizations based on their own SAW needs.

A conclusion that emerges strongly from the above finding is the importance of organizational culture in signaling to employees about what is important and valued. It has been seen earlier that the process-focus and a focus on one's attitude while working characterized the explicitly-spiritual nonprofits. An emphasis on the output or results alone may perhaps not lead to the same level of SAW experience than would be possible by focusing on the process.

6.8 The contested SAW consequences

The issue of consequences has been vigorously debated in SAW literature. Previous research has sought to empirically relate individual spirituality with job satisfaction, organizational commitment, organizational citizenship behavior, and department specific performance measures (Duchon & Plowman, 2005; Milliman et al., 2003). However, the focus on instrumental outcomes in existing studies has not addressed the concerns of the theologically inclined scholars who argue against linking spirituality to the material outcomes. This study tried to correct this lapse by seeking to quantitatively validate the outcomes of common interest to managers – job satisfaction and organizational commitment – and exploring the opinions of those who might be more sympathetic to the nonmaterial concerns.

As has been discussed in the Results chapter earlier under section 5.2, the quantitative findings were largely in line with the hypotheses that linked higher SAW scores with higher job satisfaction and organizational commitment. Both individual SAW needs and organizational SAW supplies were positively related to job satisfaction, affective organizational commitment and normative organizational commitment. This study thus lends further support to the position (Duchon & Plowman, 2005; Fry et al., 2005; Milliman et al., 2003) that SAW may have positive spin-offs for organizations and individuals.

However, none of the effects were significant for the outcome variable of Continuance Commitment that refers to an awareness of costs associated with leaving the organization. This finding is not too surprising as this variable has not found enough support in earlier studies too. Previous studies have noted that the Continuance component of Organizational Commitment consists of two separate facets: 1. low employment alternatives, and 2. high previous personal sacrifices that may be undone by the decision to move elsewhere. It has been found earlier that these two facets of continuance commitment correlated in opposite directions and may perhaps measure somewhat different constructs (Meyer & Allen, 1997:122). The six items that seek to measure Continuance Commitment too demonstrate the same ambivalence and confuse the individual's inability to leave with a commitment towards the organization (Swailes, 2002).

Further, it needs to be mentioned that the move to the nonprofit sector itself may perhaps have been a risky choice to the employees. Since commitment to a substantive value determines employment and volunteer service in the nonprofit sector (Oster, 1995), continuance may not really be an appropriate issue in the first place.

From the qualitative data, evidence was found to support the two positions of utilitarian SAW and one that served transcendental aspirations. While a few respondents forcefully associated the practice of SAW with individual and organizational improvement, a large number stuck to the position that spirituality should not be "cheapened" by being linked superficially to material outcomes. A few struck the middle path by claiming that though individual and organizational benefits shall indeed accrue but they cannot remain the sole focus of the SAW effort. The findings from this study thus lend further credence to the position that accepts individuals and organizations starting out on the spiritual path for "selfish" reasons while staying open to the possibility of the original objectives themselves undergoing a welcome change while treading the spiritual path (Benefiel, 2005). The central idea appears to be that of tolerance: an acceptance of various starting positions for the SAW journey. While for a few it could be for selfish reasons and instrumental purposes, others may perhaps be able to grasp the inner meaning and relate it not only to individual transformation but wider social upliftment as well.

In this context, it would perhaps be useful to relate this discussion with the literature on intrinsic and extrinsic religiosity and its impact on life-satisfaction in the Psychology of Religion domain. Commitment to religion and religious participation "consistently emerge as significant contributors in quality of life (QOL) indicators such as life satisfaction, happiness, and meaning in life" (Emmons, Cheung, & Tehrani, 1998:404). Other studies have found that measures of extrinsic (religion as a means to an end) religiousness generally show negative correlations with well-being, and measures of intrinsic (religion as a way of life) religiousness show positive correlations with wellbeing (see Emmons et al., 1998 for a comprehensive literature review). Further studies that go into the differences between spirituality being undertaken as a way of life versus where it is taken as a means to an end inside organizations may perhaps unravel this relationship better.

6.9 Limitations of the study

Any conclusions from this study ought to be assessed against its limitations of which a few are remarkable.

First, examination of only self-reports of the various variables cannot rule out the possibility of systematic biases. In self-reports, individuals may exaggerate or underreport owing to social desirability. So, the usual failings of the use of self-report instruments are also applicable to this study. Additionally, since spirituality is a central desirable feature of Indian culture (Sinha & Kanungo, 1997), issues relating to social desirability could not be avoided in the study.

Yet another drawback could be the measurement of attitudes and not behaviors in this study. However, this criticism is easily answered. A growing body of research testifies to the effect of individual values on actions. One recent study that looked into the effect of age on managerial values and practices in India concluded that individual values do have a strong impact on managerial practices (Mellahi & Guermat, 2004). It can thus be inferred that the individual beliefs and attitudes about spirituality too would inform their work-practices.

A far more robust argument against the study, however, is that data has been collected only from three organizations each in the two categories of nonprofits. Though the sample size was large enough to allow some generalization, it should be kept in mind that the nonprofit sector is quite broad-based and selecting only six organizations as representative of the entire sector may not be representative enough. A broader study with a larger sample size - both number of respondent and number of organizations covered - may be necessary to emerge with results that are more conclusive.

6.10 Suggestions for future research

While this study is the first to examine organizational differences in studying understandings, applications and outcomes of SAW it may have merely scratched the surface. Several issues have emerged that lend themselves to further empirical examination.

Since the study makes a case for varying SAW opportunity structures in organizations, it would be of interest to examine if the same argument holds good for the for-profit corporations as well. Various issues viz., SAW definition, religion-spirituality bifurcation, "spirit-friendly" organizational cultures, SAW expression and relationship with outcomes could then be looked at from another standpoint.

As noted earlier, the interactive effects of individual and workplace spirituality were not found to be decisive in this study. These shall need to be looked into even more rigorously to further examine this intriguing relationship.

Further, given that the data collected in this study is cross-sectional in nature, owing to the constraints of a doctoral program, future research may perhaps employ a longitudinal design to explore the organizational and individual characteristics that affect development of SAW needs and supplies in an organizational context.

References

Aga, A. (2004). Management Paradigms Beyond Profit Maximization. *Vikalpa, 29*(3), 109.

Ali, A. J., & Falcone, T. (1995). Work Ethic in the USA and Canada. *Journal of Management Development, 14*(1), 26-33.

Ashar, H., & Lane-Maher, M. (2004). Success and Spirituality in the New Business Paradigm. *Journal of Management Inquiry, 13*(3), 249-260.

Ashforth, B. E., & Pratt, M. G. (2003). Institutionalized spirituality: An oxymoron? In R. A. Giacalone & C. L. Jurkiewicz (Eds.), *Handbook of Workplace Spirituality and Organizational Performance* (pp. 93-107). Armonk, NY: M. E. Sharpe.

Ashmos, D. P., & Duchon, D. (2000). Spirituality at work: A conceptualization and measure. *Journal of Management Inquiry, 9*(2), 134-145.

Barker, E. (1995). The Scientific Study of Religion? You Must Be Joking! *Journal of Scientific Study of Religion, 34*(3), 287-310.

Bell, E., & Taylor, S. (2003). The elevation of work: Pastoral power and the New Age work ethic. *Organization, 10*(2), 329-349.

Bell, E., & Taylor, S. (2004). 'From outward bound to inward bound': The prophetic voices and discursive practices of spiritual management development. *Human Relations, 57*(4), 439-466.

Benefiel, M. (2003). Irreconcilable Foes? The Discourse of Spirituality and the Discourse of Organizational Science. *Organization, 10*(2), 383.

Benefiel, M. (2005). The second half of the journey: Spiritual leadership for organizational transformation. *The Leadership Quarterly, 16*(5), 723-747.

Biberman, J., & Whitty, M. (1997). A postmodern spiritual future for work. *Journal of Organizational Change Management, 10*(2), 130.

Biberman, J., & Whitty, M. (1999). Editorial: Twenty-First Century Spiritual Paradigms: Possibilities for Organizational Transformation. *Journal of Organizational Change Management, 12*(3), 170.

Biberman, J., Whitty, M., & Robbins, L. (1999). Lessons from Oz: Balance and wholeness in organizations. *Journal of Organizational Change Management, 12*(3), 243-253.

Bierly II, P. E., Kessler, E. H., & Christensen, E. W. (1999). Organizational learning, knowledge and wisdom. *Journal of Organizational Change Management, 13*(6), 596-618.

Boyle, M. V., & Healy, J. (2003). Balancing Mysterium and Onus: Doing Spiritual Work within an Emotion-Laden Organizational Context. *Organization, 10*(2), 351-373.

Bradley, J., & Kauanui, S. K. (2003). Comparing spirituality on three California college campuses. *Journal of Organizational Change Management, 16*(4), 448.

Brown, R. B. (2003). Organizational Spirituality: The Sceptic's Version. *Organization, 10*(2), 393-400.

Burack, E. H. (1999). Spirituality in the workplace. *Journal of Organizational Change Management, 12*(4), 280-291.

Burke, R. J., & Cooper, C. L. (2006). The new world of work and organizations: Implications for human resource management. *Human Resource Management Review, 16*(2), 83-85.

Burrell, G., & Morgan, G. (1979). *Sociological paradigms and organisational analysis.* London: Heinemann.

Casey, C. (2004). Bureaucracy re-enchanted? Spirit, experts and authority in organizations. *Organization, 11*(1), 59-79.

Cash, K. C., & Gray, G. R. (2000). A framework for accommodating religion and spirituality in the workplace. *Academy of Management Executive, 14*(3), 124-134.

Cavanagh, G. E. (1999). Spirituality for managers: context and critique. *Journal of Organizational Change Management, 12*(3), 186.

Cavanagh, G. E., & Bandsuch, M. R. (2002). Virtue as a Benchmark for Spirituality in Business. *Journal of Business Ethics, 38*(1 - 2), 109-117.

Chakraborty, S. K. (2004). Management Paradigms Beyond Profit Maximization. *Vikalpa, 29*(3), 97-117.

Clark, T. W. (2002). Spirituality without faith. *The Humanist, 62*(1), 30-35.

Collins, J. C. (2001). *Good to great: Why some companies make the leap and others don't.* New York: Harper Business.

Dean, K. L. (2004). Systems thinking's challenge to research in spirituality and religion at work: An interview with Ian Mitroff. *Journal of Organizational Change Management, 17*(1), 11-25.

Dean, K. L., Fornaciari, C. J., & McGee, J. J. (2003). Research in spirituality, religion, and work: Walking the line between relevance and legitimacy. *Journal of Organizational Change Management, 16*(4), 378-395.

Dehler, G. E., & Welsh, M. A. (1994). Spirituality and Organizational Transformation. *Journal of Managerial Psychology, 9*(6), 17-26.

Delbecq, A. L. (1999). Christian spirituality and contemporary business leadership. *Journal of Organizational Change Management, 12*(4), 345-349.

Dent, E. B., Higgins, M. E., & Wharff, D. M. (2005). Spirituality and leadership: An empirical review of definitions, distinctions, and embedded assumptions. *The Leadership Quarterly, 16*(5), 625-653.

Donaldson, L. (2001). *The Contingency Theory of Organizations.* Thousand Oaks: Sage.

Duchon, D., & Plowman, D. A. (2005). Nurturing the spirit at work: Impact on work unit performance. *The Leadership Quarterly, 16*(5), 807-833.

Duerr, M. (2004). The contemplative organization. *Journal of Organizational Change Management, 17*(1), 43-61.

Edmondson, A. (1999). Psychological Safety and Learning Behavior in Work Teams. *Administrative Science Quarterly, 44*(2), 350-383.

Edwards, J. R. (1991). Person-job fit: A conceptual integration, literature review and methodological critique. In *International Review of Industrial/Organizational Psychology* (Vol. 6, pp. 283-357). London: Wiley.

Emmons, R. A. (1999). Religion in the Psychology of Personality: An Introduction. *Journal of Personality, 67*(6), 873-888.

Emmons, R. A. (2005). Striving for the Sacred: Personal Goals, Life Meaning, and Religion. *Journal of Social Issues, 61*(4), 731-745.

Emmons, R. A., Cheung, C., & Tehrani, K. (1998). Assessing Spirituality through Personal goals: Implications for Research on Religion and Subjective Well-being. *Social Indicators Research, 45*, 391-422.

Etzioni, A. (1964). *Modern Organizations.* New Jersey: Prentice-Hall.

Fornaciari, C., & Dean, K. L. (2001). Making the quantum leap: Lessons from physics on studying spirituality and religion in organizations. *Journal of Organizational Change Management, 14*(4), 335-351.

Fornaciari, C., & Dean, K. L. (2003). Research in Spirituality, Religion, and Work: Empirical methods during the founding years. *Academy of Management Proceedings*, A1-A5.

Forray, J. M., & Stork, D. (2002). All for One: A Parable of Spirituality and Organization. *Organization, 9*(3), 497-509.

Frost, P. J. (2003). *Toxic Emotions at Work: How Compassionate Managers Handle Pain and Conflict.* Boston: Harvard Business School Press.

Frumkin, P. (2002). *On Being Nonprofit: A Conceptual and Policy Primer.* Cambridge, MA: Harvard University Press.

Fry, L. W., Vitucci, S., & Cedillo, M. (2005). Spiritual leadership and army transformation: Theory, measurement, and establishing a baseline. *The Leadership Quarterly, 16*(5), 835-862.

Garcia-Zamor, J.-C. (2003). Workplace Spirituality and Organizational Performance. *Public Administration Review, 63*(3), 355-363.

Giacalone, R. A., & Eylon, D. (2000). The Development of New Paradigm: Values, Thinkers, and Business: Initial Frameworks for a Changing Business Worldview. *American Behavioral Scientist, 43*(8), 1217-1230.

Giacalone, R. A., & Jurkiewicz, C. L. (2003a). *Handbook of workplace spirituality and organizational performance.* Armonk, NY: M. E. Sharpe.

Giacalone, R. A., & Jurkiewicz, C. L. (2003b). Toward a science of workplace spirituality. In R. A. Giacalone & C. L. Jurkiewicz (Eds.), *Handbook of workplace spirituality and organizational performance* (pp. 3-28). Armonk, NY: M. E. Sharpe.

Gibbons, P. (2000a). Spirituality at work: definitions, measures, assumptions, and validity claims. In J. Biberman & M. Whitty (Eds.), *Work and Spirit: A Reader of New Spiritual Paradigms for Organizations* (pp. 111-131). Scranton, PA: University of Scranton Press.

Gibbons, P. (2000b, Auguest 2000). *Spirituality at work: Definitions, measures, assumptions, and validity claims.* Paper presented at the Academy of Management, USA Annual Meeting, Toronto.

Goffman, E. (1961). *Asylums.* Garden City, NY: Doubleday.

Grant, D., O'Neil, K., Stephens, L. (2004). Spirituality in the Workplace: New Empirical Directions in the Study of the Sacred. *Sociology of Religion, 65*(3), 265-283.

Gull, G. A., & Doh, J. (2004). The "Transmutation" of the Organization: Toward a More Spiritual Workplace. *Journal of Management Inquiry, 13*(2), 128-139.

Gunther, M. (2001, July 9, 2001). God and Business. *Fortune, 144,* 58-80.

Hall, D. T., & Chandler, D. E. (2005). Psychological success: When the career is a *calling. Journal of Organizational Behavior, 26*(2), 155-176.

Hall, P. D., & Burke, C. B. (Writer) (2002). Historical Statistics of the United States Chapter on Voluntary, Nonprofit, and Religious Entities and Activities: Underlying Concepts, Concerns, and Opportunities [Working Paper]: Hauser Center for Nonprofit Organizations.

Hansmann, H. (1987). Political Theories of Nonprofit Organizations. In W. W. Powell (Ed.), *The Nonprofit Sector: A Research Handbook.* New Haven, Connecticut: Yale University Press.

Harvey, J. B. (2001). Reflections on books by authors who apparently are terrified about really exploring spirituality and leadership. *The Leadership Quarterly, 12*(3), 377-378.

Hefner, R. W. (1998). Multiple Modernities: Christianity, Islam, and Hinduism in a Globalizing Age. *Annual Review of Anthropology, 27,* 83-104.

Hicks, D. (2002). Spiritual and religious diversity in the workplace: Implications for leadership. *The Leadership Quarterly, 13,* 379-396.

Hill, P. C., Pargament, K., II, Hood, J. R. W., McCullough, M. E., Swyers, J. P., Larson, D. B., et al. (2000a). Conceptualizing Religion and Spirituality: Points of Commonality, Points of Departure

Conceptualizing Religion and Spirituality: Points of Commonality, Points of Departure. *Journal for the Theory of Social Behaviour, 30*(1), 51.

Hill, P. C., Pargament, K. I., Hood, R. W., McCullough, J. M. E., Swyers, J. P., Larson, D. B., et al. (2000b). Conceptualizing Religion and Spirituality: Points of Commonality, Points of Departure. *Journal for the Theory of Social Behaviour, 30*(1), 51-77.

Irwin, J. (1970). *The Felon.* Englewood Cliffs: NJ: Prentice-Hall.

Jeavons, T. H. (1998). Identifying Characteristics of "Religious" Organizations: An Exploratory Proposal. In N. J. Demerath III, Peter Dobkin Hall, Terry Schmitt & R. H. Williams (Eds.), *Sacred Companies: Organizational Aspects of Religion and Religious Aspects of Organizations* (pp. 79-95). New York: Oxford University Press.

Jex, S. M. (2002). *Organizational Psychology: A Scientist-Practitioner Approach.* New York: John Wiley & Sons.

Johansson, M., & Örndahl, M. (2003, August 14-16, 2003). *Performing Authenticity in a Context of Uncertainty* Paper presented at the 17th Nordic Conference of Business Studies Reykjavik, Iceland.

Johns, G. (2001). In praise of context. *Journal of Organizational Behavior, 22*(1), 31-42.

Jurkiewicz, C. L., & Giacalone, R. A. (2004). A Values Framework for Measuring the Impact of Workplace Spirituality on Organizational Performance. *Journal of Business Ethics, 49*(2), 129-142.

Kahnweiler, W., & Otte, F. L. (1997). In search of the soul of HRD. *Human Resource Development Quarterly, 8*(2), 171-181.

Kanter, R. M. (1968). Commitment and social organization: A study of commitment mechanisms in utopian communities. *American Sociological Review, 33,* 499-517.

King, S., & Nicol, D. M. (1999). Organizational enhancement through recognition of individual spirituality: Reflections of Jaques and Jung. *Journal of Organizational Change Management, 12*, 234-243.

Kinjerski, V. M., & Skrypnek, B. J. (2004). Defining spirit at work: Finding common ground. *Journal of Organizational Change Management, 17*(1), 26-42.

Kriger, M. P., & Hanson, B. J. (1999). A value-based paradigm for creating truly healthy organizations. *Journal of Organizational Change Management, 12*(4), 302-317.

Kriger, M. P., & Seng, Y. (2005). Leadership with inner meaning: A contingency theory of leadership based on the worldviews of five religions. *The Leadership Quarterly, 16*(5), 771-806.

Krishnakumar, S., & Neck, C. (2002). The "what", "why" and "how" of spirituality in the workplace. *Journal of Managerial Psychology, 17*(3), 153-164.

Kristof, A. (1996). Person-organization fit: an integrative review of its conceptualizations, measurement and implications. *Personnel Psychology, 49*(1), 1-49.

Kunin, T. (1955). The construction of a new type of attitude measure. *Personnel Psychology, 8*(1), 65-67.

Kurth, K. (2003). Spiritually renewing ourselves at work: Finding Meaning Through Serving In R. A. Giacalone & C. L. Jurkiewicz (Eds.), *Handbook of Workplace Spirituality and Organizational Performance* (pp. 447-460). Armonk, NY: M. E. Sharpe.

Laabs, J. L. (1995). Balancing spirituality and work. *Personnel Journal, 74*(9), 60-76.

Leech, N. L., Barrett, K. C., Morgan, G. A. (2005). *SPSS for Intermediate Statistics: Use and Interpretation* (2nd ed.). Mahwah, New Jersey: Lawrence Erlbaum Associates, Publishers.

Lichtenstein, B. B. (2000). Valid or Vacuous? A Definition and Assessment of New Paradigm Research in Management. *American Behavioral Scientist, 43*(8), 1334-1366.

Lips-Wiersma, M. (2002). Analyzing the career concerns of spiritually oriented people: Lessons for contemporary organizations. *Career Development International, 7*, 385-397.

Lips-Wiersma, M. (2002). The influence of spiritual 'meaning-making' on career behavior. *Journal of Management Development, 21*(7 - 8), 497.

Lips-Wiersma, M., & Mills, C. (2002). Coming out of the closet: Negotiating spiritual expression in the workplace. *Journal of Managerial Psychology, 17*(3), 183.

Lois, J. (1999). Socialization to Heroism: Individualism and Collectivism in a Voluntary Search and Rescue Group. *Social Psychology Quarterly, 62*(2), 117-135.

Maslow, A. H. (1998). *Maslow on Management.* New York: John Wiley.

Mellahi, K., & Guermat, C. (2004). Does age matter? An empirical examination of the effect of age on managerial values and practices in India. *Journal of World Business, 39*(2), 199-215.

Metcalf, H., & Urwick, L. (Eds.). (1941). *Dynamic Administration: The Collected Papers of Mary Parker Follett.* New York: Harper & Brothers.

Meyer, J. P., & Allen, N. J. (1997). *Commitment in the Workplace: Theory, Research, and Application.* Thousand Oaks: SAGE Publications.

Miles, M. B., & Huberman, A. M. (1994). *Qualitative Data Analysis: An expanded sourcebook* (2nd ed.). Thousand Oaks: Sage Publications.

Milliman, J., Czaplewski, A. J., & Ferguson, J. (2003). Workplace spirituality and employee work attitudes: An exploratory empirical assessment. *Journal of Organizational Change Management, 16*(4), 426-447.

Milliman, J., Ferguson, J., Trickett, D., & Condemi, B. (1999). Spirit and community at Southwest Airlines: An investigation of a spiritual values-based model. *Journal of Organizational Change Management, 12*(3), 221-233.

Mirvis, P. H. (1997). "Soul Work" in Organizations. *Organization Science, 8*(2), 193-206.

Mitroff, I. I., & Denton, E. A. (1999a). *A Spiritual Audit of Corporate America: A Hard Look at Spirituality, Religion, and Values in the Workplace.* San Francisco: Jossey-Bass Publishers.

Mitroff, I. I., & Denton, E. A. (1999b). A Study of Spirituality in the Workplace. (Cover story). *Sloan Management Review, 40*(4), 83-92.

Mohamed, A. A., Hassan, A., & Wisnieski, J. (2001). Spirituality in the workplace: A literature review. *Global Competitiveness, 9*, 644-651.

Mowday, R. T., Steers, R. M., & Porter, L. W. (1979). The measurement of organizational commitment. *Journal of Vocational Behavior, 14*(2), 224-247.

Mowday, R. T., & Sutton, R. I. (1993). Organizational behavior: Linking individuals and groups to organizational contexts. In *Annual Review of Psychology* (Vol. 44, pp. 195-229).

Neal, J. A. (1997). Spirituality in management education: A guide to resources. *Journal of Management Education, 21*(5), 121-139.

Neal, J. A. (2000). Work as service to the divine: Giving Our Gifts Selflessly and With Joy. *American Behavioral Scientist, 43*(8), 1316-1333.

Neal, J. A., & Biberman, J. (2004). Research that matters: Helping organizations integrate spiritual values and practices. *Journal of Organizational Change Management, 17*(1), 7-10.

Neal, J. A., Lichtenstein, B. M. B., & Banner, D. (1999). Spiritual perspectives on individual, organizational and societal transformation. *Journal of Organizational Change Management, 12*(3), 175-185.

Neck, C. P., & Milliman, J. F. (1994). Thought self-leadership: Finding spiritual fulfillment in organizational life. *Journal of Managerial Psychology, 9*(6), 9-16.

Oster, S. M. (1995). *Strategic Management for Nonprofit Organizations: Theory and Cases.* New York: Oxford University Press.

Paine, L. S. (2003). *Value Shift: Why Companies Must Merge Social and Financial Imperatives to Achieve Superior Performance.* New York: McGraw-Hill.

Parameshwar, S. (2005). Spiritual leadership through ego-transcendence: Exceptional responses to challenging circumstances. *The Leadership Quarterly, 16*(5), 689-722.

Pargament, K., L., Magyar-Russell, G. M., & Murray-Swank, N. A. (2005). The Sacred and the Search for Significance: Religion as a Unique Process. *Journal of Social Issues, 61*(4), 665-687.

Pava, M. L. (2003). Searching for Spirituality in All the Wrong Places. *Journal of Business Ethics, 48*(4), 393-400.

Pfeffer, J. (1998). *The Human Equation: Building Profits by Putting People First.* Boston: Harvard Business School Press.

Pielstick, C. D. (2005). Teaching Spiritual Synchronicity in a Business Leadership Class. *Journal of Management Education, 29*(1), 153-168.

Porter, L. W., & McLaughlin, G. B. (2006). Leadership and the organizational context: Like the weather? *The Leadership Quarterly, 17*(6), 559-576.

Primeaux, P., & Vega, G. (2002). Operationalizing Maslow: Religion and Flow as Business Partners. *Journal of Business Ethics, 38*(1), 97-108.

Punch, K. F. (1998). *Introduction to Social Research: Quantitative and Qualitative Approaches*: Sage Publications.

Quatro, S. A. (2002). *Organizational spiritual normativity as an influence on organizational culture and performance in Fortune 500 firms.* Unpublished Doctoral dissertation, Iowa State University.

Quatro, S. A. (2003). New Age or Age Old: Classical Management Theory and Traditional Organized Religion as underpinnings of the Contemporary Organizational Spirituality Movement. *Human Resource Development Review, 3*(3), 228-249.

Quatro, S. A. (2004). New Age or Age Old: Classical Management Theory and Traditional Organized Religion as underpinnings of the Contemporary Organizational Spirituality Movement. *Human Resource Development Review, 3*(3), 228-249.

Reave, L. (2005). Spiritual values and practices related to leadership effectiveness. *The Leadership Quarterly, 16*(5), 655-687.

Russ-Eft, D., & Preskill, H. (2001). *Evaluation in Organizations: A Systematic Approach to Enhancing Learning Performance, and Change*: Perseus Books.

Russell, R. F., & Stone, A. G. (2002). A review of servant leadership attributes: developing a practical model. *Leadership & Organization Development Journal, 23*(3), 145-157.

Schepers, C., De Gieter, S., Pepermans, R., Du Bois, C., Caers, R., & Jegers, M. (2005). How Are Employees of the Nonprofit Sector Motivated? A Research Need. *Nonprofit Management & Leadership, 16*(2), 191-208.

Schmidt-Wilk, J., Heaton, D. P., & Steingard, D. (2000). Higher education for higher consciousness: Maharishi University of Management as a model for spirituality in management education. *Journal of Management Education, 24*(5), 580-611.

Schwab, D. P. (2005). *Research Methods for Organizational Studies* (2nd ed.). Mahwah, New Jersey: Lawrence Erlbaum Associates, Publishers.

Shahjahan, R. A. (2005). Spirituality in the academy: reclaiming from the margins and evoking a transformative way of knowing the world. *International Journal of Qualitative Studies in Education, 18*(6), 685-711.

Sharma, A. (2005). *Modern Hindu Thought: An Introduction.* New Delhi: Oxford University Press.

Sheep, M. L. (2004, 9 August 2004). *Nailing Down Gossamer: A Valid Measure of the Person-Organization Fit of Workplace Spirituality.* Paper presented at the Academy of Management 2004 Annual Meeting, New Orleans.

Simons, T., & Ingram, P. (1997). Organizaiton and Ideology: Kibbutzim and hired labor, 1951-1965. *Administrative Science Quarterly, 42*, 784-813.

Sinha, J. B. P. (1997). A Cultural Perspective on Organizational Behavior in India. In P. C. Earley & M. Erez (Eds.), *New Perspectives on International Industrial/Organizational Psychology.* San Francisco: The New Lexington Press.

Sinha, J. B. P., & Kanungo, R. N. (1997). Context Sensitivity and Balancing in Indian Organizational behavior. *International Journal of Psychology, 32*(2), 93-105.

Smith, P. C. (1975). *The Job Descriptive Index.* Bowling Green, Ohio: Bowling Green State University.

Speck, B. W. (2005). What is Spirituality? *New Directions for Teaching and Learning, 104*(Winter), 3-13.

Spector, P. E. (1994). Using self-report questionnaires in OB research. *Journal of Organizational Behavior, 15*, 385-392.

Spector, P. E. (1997). *Job Satisfaction: Application, Assessment, Causes, and Consequences.* Thousand Oaks: SAGE Publications.

Svejenova, S. (2005). 'The Path with the Heart': Creating the Authentic Career. *Journal of Management Studies, 42*(5), 947-974.

Swailes, S. (2002). Organizational commitment: a critique of the construct and measures. *International Journal of Management Reviews, 4*(2), 155–178.

Tischler, L. (1999). The growing interest in spirituality in business. *Journal of Organizational Change Management, 12*(4), 273-279.

Tischler, L. (1999). The growing interest in spirituality in business: A long-term socio-economic explanation. *Journal of Organizational Change Management, 12*, 273-280.

Tourish, D., & Pinnington, A. (2002). Transformational leadership, corporate cultism and the spirituality paradigm: An unholy trinity in the workplace? *Human Relations, 55*(2), 147-172.

Vaill, P. (2000). Introduction to Spirituality for Business Leadership. *Journal of Management Inquiry, 9*(2), 115.

Vaill, P. B. (1998). *Spirited Leading and Learning: Process Wisdom for a New Age.* San Francisco: Jossey-Bass Publishers.

Vaughan, D. (1992). Theory Elaboration: the Heuristics of Case Analysis. In C. B. Ragin, H. (Ed.), *What is A Case: Exploring the Foundations of Social Inquiry.* Cambridge, MA Cambridge University Press.

Waddock, S. (1999). Linking community and spirit: A commentary and some propositions. *Journal of Organizational Change Management, 12*, 332-345.

Wagner-Marsh, F., & Conley, J. (1999). The fourth wave: the spiritually-based firm. *Journal of Organizational Change Management, 12*(4), 292.

Weiss, D. J., Dawis, R. V., England, G. W., & Lofquist, L. H. (1967). *Manual for the Minnesota Satisfaction Questionnaire.* Minneapolis: University of Minnesota.

Westerman, J. W., & Cyr, L. A. (2004). An Integrative Analysis of Person-Organization Fit Theories. *International Journal of Selection and Assessment, 12*(3), 252-261.

Wittmer, D. (1991). Serving the People or Serving for Pay: Reward Preferences Among Government, Hybrid Sector and Business Managers. *Public Productivity and Management Review, 14*(4), 369-383.

Wright, J. D., & Hamilton, R. F. (1978). Work Satisfaction and Age: Some Evidence for the 'Job Change' Hypothesis. *Social Forces, 56*(4), 1140-1158.

Yalom, I. D. (1980). *Existential Psychotherapy*. New York: Basic Books.

Yin, R. K. (1981). *Case Study Research, Design and Methods*. California: Sage Publications.

Zinnbauer, B. J., Pargament, K. I., & Scott, A. B. (1999). The emerging meanings of religiousness and spirituality: Problems and Prospects. *Journal of Personality, 67*(6), 889-919.

Appendices

Appendix 1
SPIRITUALITY AT WORK
<u>SURVEY</u>

'Spirituality at Work' is a concept that has recently caught scholars' attention in academic circles. Literature suggests that spirituality at work could be looked at in three dimensions:

1. <u>Integrity and Wholeness</u> implies that individuals try to express all parts of themselves at work and that the organization places an emphasis upon the individuals leading a non-fragmented life.
2. <u>Meaningful work</u> involves purposeful work that is valued by individuals not just for its instrumental outcomes but as one that provides them with a sense of purpose.
3. <u>Larger than oneself</u> dimension means the organizational members connecting with their community and sharing a common identity. It could work at two levels: one, within the organization and two, beyond the organization at the level of the community in which the organization finds itself. At both levels it would imply being a part of a community larger than oneself and contributing towards it.

We are exploring the extent to which individuals desire these three dimensions of spirituality at work, the extent to which enabling conditions are provided by their current organizations and the attendant consequences. We hope to use the data we collect to improve our understanding of the practice of spirituality at work and make recommendations about its impact on individuals and organizations.

In the pages that follow, please try to respond based on your personal experiences inside the organization. Be assured that your response will be held in strict confidence, and be used only for the intended purpose of advancing academic knowledge through research.

Your Name: _____

Today's Date: _____

Demographic Information:

Age:_____ years   Prior work-ex.: ↑Yes↑No

Sex: ↑Male↑Female   If yes, where and in what capacity: _____

Education: _____

High School: _____   Why of change: _____

Graduation degree in: _____   _____

Post-graduation degree in: _____   _____

Doctorate in: _____   _____

Highest degree Area: _____   _____

Organization Name: _____   _____

Deptt/Unit/Work-group: _____   _____

Years in Organization:_____   _____

Joined in year:_____   _____

Years in current role:_____   _____

Questionnaire
Part I
INDIVIDUAL PREFERENCES

INSTRUCTIONS:

Using the scale shown below, circle the number that best describes your response to each statement.
Each statement aids us in understanding better how individuals feel about themselves and their organization.

EXAMPLE:

1	2	3	4	5
Strongly Disagree	Disagree	Neutral	Agree	Strongly Agree

1 2 3 4 5	1. I would prefer if people are mutually respected at my workplace.
1 2 3 4 5	2. It is important for me to connect with others in my organization.
1 2 3 4 5	3. I would prefer that my work provides a sense of purpose to me.
1 2 3 4 5	4. Working cooperatively with others should be encouraged at my workplace.
1 2 3 4 5	5. I should be able to make a contribution to the larger community around me at my workplace.
1 2 3 4 5	6. It is important for me to experience joy in work.
1 2 3 4 5	7. I prefer to share my convictions at my workplace.
1 2 3 4 5	8. It is important to me that I am able to express myself through my work.
1 2 3 4 5	9. I would prefer if my organization encourages a strong sense of community.
1 2 3 4 5	10. It is important to me that people support each other personally in my organization.
1 2 3 4 5	11. My organization should enable me to integrate my spiritual life with my work life.
1 2 3 4 5	12. My work should mean more than its material benefits to me.
1 2 3 4 5	13. I would ideally like to utilize all my talents at work.
1 2 3 4 5	14. It is important for me that my work contributes significantly to the meaningfulness of my life.
1 2 3 4 5	15. I would prefer if my personal life is integrated with my professional life.
1 2 3 4 5	16. I would prefer that my organization genuinely cares about its members.
1 2 3 4 5	17. It is important to me for my organization to provide an environment to lead an integrated life.
1 2 3 4 5	18. I prefer if the people I interact with experience joy as a result of my work.
1 2 3 4 5	19. I would prefer to express my total intelligence at work.
1 2 3 4 5	20. It is important for me to express my total feelings at work.
1 2 3 4 5	21. It is important for me to feel energized by the work I do.
1 2 3 4 5	22. I would prefer to speak my mind at work.
1 2 3 4 5	23. I desire to act in ways consistent with my values at my organization.
1 2 3 4 5	24. It is important to me that my work is connected to the larger social good of my community.
1 2 3 4 5	25. The work I do should be connected to what I think is important in life.
1 2 3 4 5	26. I would prefer not feeling drained out by the end of the work-day.
1 2 3 4 5	27. It is important to me that my work appear to be my calling.

2

ORGANIZATIONAL CONDITIONS

INSTRUCTIONS:

Using the scale shown below, circle the number that best describes your response to each statement.

Each statement aids us in understanding better how individuals feel about themselves and their organization.

EXAMPLE:

1	2	3	4	5
Strongly Disagree	Disagree	Neutral	Agree	Strongly Agree

1 2 3 4 5	1. My present organization encourages a strong sense of community.
1 2 3 4 5	2. This organization provides an environment for me to lead an integrated life.
1 2 3 4 5	3. Sharing of one's convictions is not encouraged at my workplace.
1 2 3 4 5	4. I am able to express my total intelligence at work.
1 2 3 4 5	5. I find it difficult to connect with others in this organization.
1 2 3 4 5	6. My work does mean more than its material benefits to me.
1 2 3 4 5	7. I believe the organization genuinely cares about its members.
1 2 3 4 5	8. I do not see a connection between my work and the larger social good of my community.
1 2 3 4 5	9. I am unable to express my total feelings at work.
1 2 3 4 5	10. I do feel drained out by the end of the work-day.
1 2 3 4 5	11. I believe people support each other personally in this organization.
1 2 3 4 5	12. I do not see myself making a contribution to the larger community around me.
1 2 3 4 5	13. I believe the people I interact with experience joy as a result of my work.
1 2 3 4 5	14. I am able to utilize my talents at work in this organization.
1 2 3 4 5	15. I feel energized by my work.
1 2 3 4 5	16. I work in an environment where people are mutually respected.
1 2 3 4 5	17. My work appears to be my calling.
1 2 3 4 5	18. My work contributes significantly to the meaningfulness of my life.
1 2 3 4 5	19. I feel constrained in expressing myself through my work.
1 2 3 4 5	20. My work provides a sense of purpose to me.
1 2 3 4 5	21. I am able to speak my mind at work.
1 2 3 4 5	22. Working cooperatively with others is not valued enough in this organization.
1 2 3 4 5	23. The work I do is somehow not connected to what I think is important in life.
1 2 3 4 5	24. My organization enables me to integrate my spiritual life with my work life.
1 2 3 4 5	25. I find that my personal life is quite distinct from my professional life.
1 2 3 4 5	26. I find it difficult to act in ways consistent with my values at work.
1 2 3 4 5	27. I experience joy in my work.

Questionnaire
Part II

Listed below is a series of statements that represent possible feelings that individuals may have about the organization for which they are working. With respect to your own feelings about the particular organization for which you are now working, please indicate the extent of your agreement or disagreement with each statement by circling a number from 1 to 5.

EXAMPLE:

1	2	3	4	5
Strongly Disagree	Disagree	Neutral	Agree	Strongly Agree

1 2 3 4 5	1. I would not leave my organization right now because I have a sense of obligation to the people in it.
1 2 3 4 5	2. I would be very happy to spend the rest of my life with this organization.
1 2 3 4 5	3. It would be very hard for me to leave my organization right now.
1 2 3 4 5	4. I owe a great deal to my organization.
1 2 3 4 5	5. Right now, staying with my organization is a matter of desire rather than a necessity.
1 2 3 4 5	6. This organization deserves my loyalty.
1 2 3 4 5	7. I do not feel a strong sense of belonging to my organization.
1 2 3 4 5	8. One of the major reasons I continue to work for this organization is that leaving would require considerable personal sacrifice; another organization may not match the overall benefits I have here.
1 2 3 4 5	9. I do not feel any obligation to remain with my current organization.
1 2 3 4 5	10. Too much of my life would be disrupted if I decided I wanted to leave my organization right now.
1 2 3 4 5	11. I do not feel like "part of a family" at my organization.
1 2 3 4 5	12. One of the few negative consequences of leaving this organization would be the scarcity of available alternatives.
1 2 3 4 5	13. Even if it were to my advantage, I do not feel it would be right to leave my organization now.
1 2 3 4 5	14. I really feel as if this organization's problems are my own.
1 2 3 4 5	15. The organization has a great deal of personal meaning for me.

4

INSTRUCTIONS:

Using the scale shown below, circle the number that best describes your response to each statement.

Each statement aids us in understanding better how individuals feel about themselves and their organization.

EXAMPLE:

1	2	3	4	5
Strongly Disagree	Disagree	Neutral	Agree	Strongly Agree

1 2 3 4 5	1. I feel satisfied with my chances for improvement in material conditions here.
1 2 3 4 5	2. My superior shows little interest in the feelings of subordinates.
1 2 3 4 5	3. I am not satisfied with the benefits I receive.
1 2 3 4 5	4. Supervisors here are usually fair.
1 2 3 4 5	5. The benefits we receive are as good as other comparable organizations.
1 2 3 4 5	6. There is really too little chance for advancement on my job.
1 2 3 4 5	7. I often feel that I do not know what is going on with the organization.
1 2 3 4 5	8. When I do a good job, I receive the recognition for it that I should receive.
1 2 3 4 5	9. Many of our rules and procedures make doing a good job difficult.
1 2 3 4 5	10. I like the people I work with.
1 2 3 4 5	11. I feel I have to work harder at my job because the people I work with are unwilling to take charge.
1 2 3 4 5	12. I feel a sense of pride in doing my job.
1 2 3 4 5	13. I feel I derive adequate material benefits for the work I do.
1 2 3 4 5	14. Those who do well on the job stand a fair chance of advancing in this organization.
1 2 3 4 5	15. I sometimes feel my job is meaningless.
1 2 3 4 5	16. I do not feel that the work I do is appreciated enough.
1 2 3 4 5	17. I am expected to do things I do not enjoy doing.
1 2 3 4 5	18. Work assignments are not fully explained in our organization.

Annexure 2
"Spirituality at Work" Interview Protocol

Organizational Choices and incidents
1. When and why did you choose to join [name of the organization]?
2. What other options could you have exercised then had it not been for [name of the organization]?
3. What were your initial impressions about [name of the organization]?
4. Could you relate a few experiences illustrating the organization's culture from your early days here?
5. What were your feelings about these incidents or how did you react to them then?
6. What is it about your work that you value most?
7. Could you tell us what are the basic values that guide your life?
8. What are the values that you practice at work?
9. Would you agree that it is possible for one's values to be compromised in an organization's reality? In your experience has it happened to someone here?

Organizational issues
10. What do you like most about your organization?
11. What would you feel are the benefits of staying in this organization?
12. How could these be improved upon?
13. What makes you most connected to this organization?
14. Why would you *want to stay* in this organization?
15. Why would you feel that you *ought to* continue with this organization?
16. What factors, if any, would convince you to leave this organization?

Spirituality
17. What does the term spirituality mean to you?
18. How important is it to you personally?
19. Some people say that their understanding of spirituality has changed over a period of time. Has yours too evolved during your stay in [name of the organization]? If yes, how?
20. Looking back at your tenure in this organization, have your perceptions about the organization itself changed? If yes, how? What has led to such a change?

Spirituality at work
21. Would you consider spirituality to be relevant to the workplace?
22. Is spirituality an appropriate topic for discussion in the workplace?
23. Should spirituality be dealt with outside of the workplace?
24. Why?
25. How could spirituality be practiced at work?
26. What all behaviors could contribute to making the workplace spiritual?
27. What all behaviors would inhibit the practice of spirituality at work?
28. Which organizational features would encourage the practice of spirituality at work?
29. Which organizational features would inhibit the practice of spirituality at work?
30. In sum, would you feel that spirituality is practiced in your organization?
31. Could you cite some specific incidents that illustrate the practice of spirituality at work?
32. What, in your view, could be the probable consequences of spirituality at work?
33. Could there also be some negative consequences of practicing spirituality at work?
34. Could there also be some consequences of *not* practicing spirituality at work?
35. Do you think there could be some more issues left unaddressed in our interview that would shed more light on the phenomenon of spirituality at work?

Breinigsville, PA USA
06 February 2011
254922BV00007B/46/P